HOW TO POWER TUNE
MINI
ON A **SMALL** BUDGET

– To Alison, a lifelong Mini fan –

www.veloce.co.uk

First published in 2001 by Veloce Publishing Limited, Veloce House, Parkway Farm Business Park, Middle Farm Way, Poundbury, Dorchester DT1 3AR, England. Fax 01305 250479 / e-mail info@veloce.co.uk / web www.veloce.co.uk or www.velocebooks.com.
Reprinted 2004. Revised and updated edition published 2005 and reprinted March 2017. ISBN: 978-1-787110-87-8; UPC: 6-36847-01087-4.
© 2001, 2004, 2005 and 2017 Des Hammill and Veloce Publishing. All rights reserved. With the exception of quoting brief passages for the purpose of review, no part of this publication may be recorded, reproduced or transmitted by any means, including photo-copying, without the written permission of Veloce Publishing Ltd. Throughout this book logos, model names and designations, etc, have been used for the purposes of identification, illustration and decoration. Such names are the property of the trademark holder as this is not an official publication. Readers with ideas for automotive books, or books on other transport or related hobby subjects, are invited to write to the editorial director of Veloce Publishing at the above address. British Library Cataloguing in Publication Data – A catalogue record for this book is available from the British Library. Typesetting, design and page make-up all by Veloce Publishing Ltd on Apple Mac. Printed and bound by CPI Group (UK) Ltd, Croydon, CR0 4YY.

HOW TO POWER TUNE
MINI
ON A **SMALL** BUDGET

Des Hammill

ENLARGED EDITION
NOW IN COLOUR!

VELOCE PUBLISHING
THE PUBLISHER OF FINE AUTOMOTIVE BOOKS

Veloce *SpeedPro* books –

978-1-903706-59-6

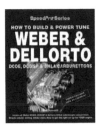

978-1-903706-75-6

978-1-903706-76-3

978-1-903706-99-2

978-1-845840-21-1

978-1-845840-73-0

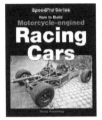

978-1-845841-23-2

978-1-845841-86-7

978-1-845841-87-4

978-1-845842-07-9

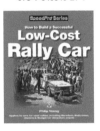

978-1-845842-08-6

978-1-845842-62-8

978-1-845842-89-5

978-1-845842-97-0

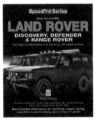

978-1-845843-15-1

978-1-845843-55-7

978-1-845844-33-2

978-1-845844-38-7

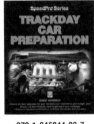

978-1-845844-83-7

978-1-845846-15-2

978-1-845848-33-0

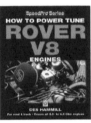

978-1-845848-68-2

978-1-845848-69-9

978-1-845849-60-3

978-1-845840-19-8

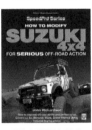

978-1-787110-92-2

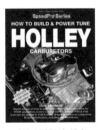

978-1-787110-47-2

978-1-903706-94-7

978-1-787110-87-8

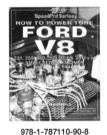

978-1-787110-90-8

978-1-787110-01-4

978-1-901295-26-9

978-1-845841-62-1

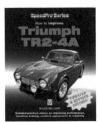

978-1-787110-91-5

978-1-787110-88-5

978-1-903706-78-7

Contents

SPEEDPRO SERIES

Using this book & essential information

USING THIS BOOK

Throughout this book the text assumes that you, or your contractor, will have a workshop manual (specific to your Mini, the engine and other major components to be worked on) to follow for complete detail on dismantling, reassembly, adjustment procedure, clearances, torque figures, etc. This book's default is the standard manufacturer's specification for your Mini model or component type so, if a procedure is not described, a measurement not given, a torque figure ignored, you can assume that the standard manufacturer's procedure or specification needs to be used.

You'll find it helpful to read the whole book before you start work or give instructions to your contractor. This is because a modification or change in specification in one area will often cause the need for changes in other areas. Get the whole picture so that you can finalize specification and component requirements as far as is possible before any work begins.

ESSENTIAL INFORMATION

This book contains information on practical procedures; however, this information is intended only for those with the qualifications, experience, tools and facilities to carry out the work in safety and with appropriately high levels of skill. Whenever working on a car or component, remember that your personal safety must ALWAYS be your FIRST consideration. The publisher, author, editors and retailer of this book cannot accept any responsibility for personal injury or mechanical damage which results from using this book, even if caused by errors or omissions in the information given. If this disclaimer is unacceptable to you, please return the pristine book to your retailer who will refund the purchase price.

In the text of this book "**Warning!**" means that a procedure could cause personal injury and "**Caution!**" that there is danger of mechanical damage if appropriate care is not taken. However, be aware that we cannot possibly foresee every possibility of danger in every circumstance.

Please note that changing component specification by modification is likely to void warranties and also to absolve manufacturers from any responsibility in the event of component failure and the consequences of such failure.

Increasing the engine's power will place additional stress on engine components and on the car's complete driveline: this may reduce service life and increase the frequency of breakdown. An increase in engine power, and therefore the vehicle's performance, will mean that your vehicle's braking and suspension systems will need to be kept in perfect condition and uprated as appropriate. It is also usually necessary to inform the vehicle's insurers of any changes to the vehicle's specification.

The importance of cleaning a component thoroughly before working on it cannot be overstressed. Always keep your working area and tools as clean as possible. Whatever specialist cleaning fluid or other chemicals you use, be sure to follow - completely - manufacturer's instructions and if you are using petrol (gasoline) or paraffin (kerosene) to clean parts, take every precaution necessary to protect your body and to avoid all risk of fire.

Introduction & Acknowledgements

INTRODUCTION

This book deals with road going Minis for which an improvement in engine performance is wanted, but at low cost, without too much mechanical work and with reasonable fuel economy too. Most people want cost-effective 'bolt-on' or 'bolt-in' performance enhancements and that's what this book features.

In the context of this book 'bolt-on' means things like inlet manifolds, exhaust manifolds and cylinder heads and 'bolt-in' means components that are fitted inside the engine such as a camshaft or a timing chain.

There are no very expensive parts to buy for any of the alterations suggested in this book, the use of standard readily available parts being recommended wherever possible though a few parts just have to be aftermarket components.

Engines are 'packages' in the sense that no one thing is the magic ingredient that is going to transform the engine from a docile standard unit into high performance engine. There are a number of things that have to be done to an engine to get the most out of it, and they're detailed in this book in basic order. To skip a recommended alteration is to miss out on some power, and perhaps economy, somewhere along the line.

The modifications detailed in this book are not very time consuming. Nevertheless, you can undertake the work (or have it done for you) with the certain knowledge that the results will be very acceptable, so your time and money will have been well spent.

Surprisingly - after so many years of A-Series engine use - there is still a huge amount of confusion about what to do and what not to do to these engines to improve performance. It's all too easy to spend a lot of money on an engine which then does not perform as expected. Often the reason for this is that the engine is simply not tuned (adjusted) correctly once it is running. Make no mistake about this, a good tune-up to the right specifications (especially ignition timing!) is vital ...

This book also covers likely scenarios for when things go wrong. Anyone with a reasonable amount of mechanical knowledge will be able to check and in most cases rectify problems themselves. There are no tricks with any of this work, just a logical sequence of events to be carried out with care.

The A+ range of engines, which means 998cc or 1275cc engines made after 1980, are the best A-Series engines to use because of the improvements made to them, and because they are the most recent (so have fewer fatigued parts). The MG Metro engines were the most powerful naturally aspirated A-series engines (72bhp). The factory tested these engines to 7000rpm and they were very reliable. The 1275cc Cooper S engines, by comparison, produced only 67bhp.

Final testing of the MG Metro Turbo engine involved the technology being applied to the North/South versions of these engines as fitted to Morris Marinas. The reason for doing this was that with the boost at a maximum of 9psi, the East/West gearboxes were not holding up. The Marina cars were able to have the B-Series gearboxes fitted to them for the trials, and they could take the extra power. The 4.5psi that the MG Metro Turbo cars all had was settled on after the trials as the cylinder head gaskets started to become unreliable. Power output was reported to be 115bhp.

Using the newest and lowest mileage engine you can find as a base unit is always a good move. It's pretty hard to beat a low mileage engine as a basis for a high performance road going engine if the engine is not going to be completely rebuilt. In many instances, buying a late model engine out of a low mileage wrecked or rusted out car represents the best possible value for money as virtually nothing has to be done to the basic short assembly of the engine. The clutch plate will have to be replaced, the simplex timing chain replaced and, perhaps, the camshaft.

Some of you outside the UK will have to rebuild the engine you have, but parts are reasonably cheap and almost always readily available too.

Buying a second engine and gearbox (transmission) and then preparing them to the level you require before swapping the complete engine/gearbox unit is quite a good idea. This method means that the car will only be off the road for a day (if that), yet all of the vital aspects of the engine will have been dealt with.

You can also consult a reputable engine reconditioning business for details of exchange short blocks or having your own engine rebuilt. The rebuilding of an A-Series engine is very straightforward and there are no particular complications. Many engine reconditioners have exchange short blocks available which have been rebored, had new pistons and rings fitted, new main and big end bearings fitted, and a crankshaft grind, and the connecting rods have had their big ends resized. Also, new little end bushes (where applicable), the top of the block machined to clean it up, new camshaft bearings, a new camshaft and lifters, a new oil pump, timing chain and all new gaskets. To all intents and purposes engines which have been thoroughly and properly rebuilt can be considered to be new and capable of giving excellent service. Usually the cost of a rebuilt short engine is not too horrendous.

Engines that have recently been reconditioned but for one reason or another have ended up for sale can also be excellent bargains.

What needs to be treated with great caution is an engine that is claimed to be rebuilt but which has only had a new set of rings and a cylinder bore hone and little else. While honing the bores and fitting new piston rings is all well and good, it is only good if the bores are on size and the piston ring grooves are in as new condition. Many are not, yet they are rebuilt when they shouldn't be. Such engines are usually a complete waste of money because they rarely last and they never ever produce original power. Unfortunately there are a lot of these engines around. Remember that if an engine is going to be altered for high performance the base unit must be sound otherwise failure is almost assured.

For those who want to do the full engine rebuild themselves, there is another SpeedPro book that deals specifically with four cylinder in-line engine rebuilding and the checking of parts: *How To Blueprint & Build A 4-Cylinder Short Block For High Performance* by Des Hammill.

Piston ring wear and main bearing wear are the Achilles heels of the A-Series engine. It is, for example, quite possible (and common) for an A-Series to have 'on size' (in tolerance) pistons and completely unworn bores and yet be a 'smoker' (oil burner). The piston rings are almost always the problem in this situation and replacement is the only solution. The later design, three piece (more efficient design than a one piece ring) oil control ring is part of the solution to this problem on later A+ engines. Be aware that many small bore replacement piston sets still come with the less efficient one piece oil control ring: one piece oil control rings do not last as long as the three piece A+ oil control rings.

For those who are wondering, the maximum number of standard engine parts can be retained on a road going engine because the stresses involved are never the same as in a racing situation. In far too many instances money is wasted on special parts in areas where there is little or no gain for the money and, while the alternative parts might well be much stronger than the standard parts, the extra strength is not actually needed on the road. The recommendation is to spend money on specialist parts only when you really need to.

Of course, there are a few areas which do need non-standard parts in the interests of general reliability and overall longevity, but they are few and far between. In fact, there are only two areas which fall into this category and they're the clutch and the simplex (single row) timing chain on ALL of these engines.

All too often a different carburettor and inlet manifold is fitted in an effort to dramatically improve the engine's overall performance, but the results are usually poor or disappointing. In fact, in most instances, the standard single SU carburetion is enough for any road going application provided certain aspects of the tuning of these carburettors is attended to. The single standard $1^1/_2$in or $1^3/_4$in SU on any road going engine should be the last thing to be changed, not the first!

While some Mini engines were originally equipped with twin SUs, there are problems (to do with the linkage and linkage wear) with carburettor synchronisation. Twin SUs can work well, but they do not offer any significant advantage over a suitably-sized single SU. The recommendation is to stay with a single SU for any road going application. There is no doubt that for simplicity and good overall engine performance, a single SU is virtually impossible to beat.

IMPORTANT EQUIPMENT

Once all the modifications suggested in this book have been made, the engine will need to be tuned so that all of the components are working correctly together. To do this work properly you'll need several items of equipment, as follows. You could hire it if you don't want to buy.

A stroboscopic timing light ('strobe light') to check and then set the ignition timing in relation to a correctly marked crankshaft pulley/damper and pointer.

A multimeter is an essential piece of equipment because with it the resistance of plug wires (HT leads) can be checked. Also battery voltage when the engine is not running (12.4-12.8 volts for a fully charged battery), and when the engine is running (13.4-13.8

volts normally, but 14.0 is possible) which indicates that the alternator and the battery are working correctly. All manner of circuit checking can be done with a multimeter.

A compression gauge will tell you roughly how good the engine is and whether or not there is any difference between cylinders. It will also tell you by how much the engine has improved after being modified and if the engine is retested at a later stage you will have some datum readings to refer to. Any reduction in compression means that something is not quite right.

ENGINE TESTING

If you carry out the following tests before you make any modifications to your car's engine, you'll be able to compare the results with the post-modification performance to see what improvement has been gained. By using these tests, you'll also be able to measure the value of individual modifications like carburettor needle changes.

Always repeat tests several times to make sure that the results are consistent.

Measuring acceleration

Acceleration can be easily tested on a suitable road. One of the simplest tests is to check the 0 to 50 or 0 to 70 miles per hour time (or to whatever speed is legal). This can be achieved with reasonable accuracy using a stopwatch and the car's own speedometer (even if it is not all that accurate, it will be consistently inaccurate).

The car is driven from the standing start (using the same starting revs each time) and taken up to the end of the power curve in each gear before changing to the next ratio.

The aim here is to check how many seconds it takes for the car to get to the same chosen speedo reading over several runs. It's quite remarkable how accurate this test is on a straight and level stretch of road. Most people can drive the car that they are used to quite consistently, and if a change is made to the engine or its settings the improvement or worsening in acceleration can be measured by part seconds or, maybe, whole seconds.

The car's acceleration in top gear from 40mph to 70mph can also be timed. This involves driving along steadily at 40mph in top gear and then pressing the accelerator pedal to the floor and starting a stopwatch as you do so. When the speedo needle hits 70mph, stop the watch. The time taken gives the mid-range performance capability of the engine.

Measuring fuel consumption

Fill the fuel tank right up until the pump clicks off, record the mileage and the amount of fuel put into the car and then drive it in the normal manner. When the tank is almost empty, fill the tank right up to the top until the pump clicks off. Record the mileage and exactly how much fuel it took to fill the tank. The miles covered divided by the quantity of fuel gives you the average miles per gallon. A similar test can be carried out on the motorway at the speed that you normally drive at.

ACKNOWLEDGEMENTS

I would like to acknowledge the valuable assistance given to me by David R Smith (Smithy). He has an encyclopaedic memory when it comes to Minis, and his help has been invaluable.

Chapter 1

Engine condition

USED ENGINES

There is no point, whatsoever, in trying to use an A-Series engine in a high performance road going application if the engine is not mechanically sound to start with. If the engine is a genuine low mileage one, the chances are that it will be sound and will be quite satisfactory as the base for a higher performance unit. Unless an engine is actually checked for wear and component damage there will always be some risk of engine failure. However, if the unit is a low mileage one, most people will take the risk and hope that they get reasonable service out of the particular engine.

Fortunately, good A-Series engines at reasonable prices are not too difficult to find, especially in the UK. Nevertheless, some engines are going to be better value than others, so shop around. When an engine that appears suitable is found the first thing to do - before you pay for it - is to remove the cylinder head and check

that the bores have no wear at all. Any evidence of a bore ridge usually means high miles or that the engine has been used for lots of short journeys with the choke on. Don't use an engine with perceptible bore wear. Well looked after A-Series engines can have near perfect bores even after 50,000 miles/80,000 kilometres, which says a lot for the engine.

Be aware though that just because an engine has an unworn bore it does not mean it's perfect with regard to piston ring sealing. Unfortunately, the A-Series engine has a reputation for burning a bit of oil even when in good condition. Replacing the rings does not always remove the oil burning problem, although replacing the rings is the solution (if the new rings seat correctly). One of the ways of helping to prevent an engine that has had new rings fitted to it from burning oil is to initially run the engine on 'straight' 20/50 motor oil (no additives) for 500 miles, or so. After the initial running-in

period of about 500 miles a friction modified oil or any other high quality alternative oil can be used.

If any engine you find has significant bore wear, the chances are that it will not last long in a high performance application and will also never deliver maximum engine power and maximum fuel economy. There is absolutely no doubt that there is no substitute for perfectly round virtually unworn bores in any high performance engine. Any engine that has no bore wear can have new piston rings fitted to it and piston to bore sealing restored to original specification, providing the pistons are in good condition.

An engine with perceptible bore wear will soon need a re-bore, together with new pistons and rings. Further, an engine which has worn bores will use oil and likely as not smoke; it'll also probably have a worn bottom end. This could mean that the bearing shells, crankshaft journals, and oil pump are not in good condition.

The A-Series engine is a long stroke (the distance the piston travels) design and is prone to bearing and crankshaft journal wear when subjected to high rpm. One of the main causes of excessive bearing and crankshaft journal wear, however, is dirt in the oil. If an engine has had infrequent oil changes the chances are that the bearing shells will have dirt particles embedded in them and they will continue to wear away the crankshaft journals - even after the oil has been changed ...

Many scrapyards will allow the cylinder head to be removed provided you take a new cylinder head gasket to give them in the event you don't buy the engine. If the engine is suitable, you have a bargain: if not, don't buy it - you've only lost a little time and the cost of an inexpensive gasket. It's better to do this than taking a chance and ending up with a worn out and essentially useless engine!

Before any secondhand engine or shortblock is bought, it pays to remove the flywheel and see what the condition of the crankshaft taper is (see clutch chapter) because, if it's damaged at all, the engine is useless to you. If possible, find out what the crankshaft taper is like before handing over money! Flywheels are relatively disposable because they are easy to replace; the crankshaft taper condition is the major issue.

RECONDITIONED SHORTBLOCKS

An alternative is to buy a reconditioned engine shortblock (the cylinder block and its internal components) from a reputable engine reconditioner or an engine parts supplier. Your old engine shortblock (or a scrapyard shortblock) can be part-exchanged or, often, you can buy recon short blocks without an exchange being necessary. Good recon units are, effectively, new engines because they will have been rebored, new replacement oversize pistons and rings fitted (maximum recommended oversize bore is plus 0.060in), new bearing shells fitted to the crankshaft and the crankshaft reground undersize (if necessary). New camshaft bearings will have been fitted as will a new oil pump. The camshaft will usually be new or reground and the lifters will be new or refaced. The timing chain will be new and there will be new gaskets and locking tabs fitted throughout the unit. The block will have also been thoroughly cleaned inside and out. When reconditioning is done properly, the engine will give excellent service. Note that any A-Series engine that is rebored should be given 0.002-0.0023in/0.050-0.058mm piston to bore clearance.

An engine which has had new rings fitted to the existing pistons, a bore hone and, perhaps, new bearing shells fitted is not a 'reconditioned' engine: there's a bit more to it than that.

If you don't mind losing the use of your car for a few days, it's quite feasible to have your own engine rebuilt by a reconditioner but using the appropriate heavy duty/higher performance like a duplex timing chain and an MG 1300 Metro camshaft (or similar). This work will cost money but, all things being equal, the engine will be exactly right from day one and will give years of reliable service.

Chapter 2

Which engine?

1275CC A+

There is no doubt that the 1275cc A-Series engine - preferably an A+ unit - has the potential to produce the most power of all of the A-Series engines available. The reliability of these engines (with standard parts in good condition) is virtually guaranteed up to 7000rpm. The two things that will eventually let such an engine down are the clutch plate and the standard timing chain. Both problems are easily avoided by using alternative components which are readily available and reasonably inexpensive.

Caution! Boring a 1275cc engine oversize beyond the usual maximum is not recommended for road use and can be the cause of block related problems. Avoid problems by staying within recognised bore oversizes which are plus 0.010in, plus 0.020in, plus 0.030in, plus 0.040in and plus 0.060in. You can use original equipment pistons or normal aftermarket alternatives. Forget about

boring out a standard but worn 1275cc block to 1380cc just to get extra capacity, the modification can be more trouble than it's worth (boring into the oil way drillings in the block or the water pump securing holes on the front cylinder) and for no increase in useable power for a road car.

As an identifying feature all A+ 1275 engines have slot-drive oil pumps and this system is the most reliable of the three drives used on A-Series engines - pin-drive first, star-drive second and, finally, slot-drive. It's recommended that an engine which has covered 50,000 miles/80,000 kilometres, or more, has a new oil pump fitted. **Caution!** - Oil pumps do wear and can be the cause of low oil pressure in these engines. The other cause of low oil pressure is worn or damaged main and big end bearing shells or worn or damaged crankshaft journals (not enough oil changes).

Early pre A+ 1275cc engines had smaller diameter big end journals and,

while it's often claimed that Cooper S crankshafts like this are the ultimate, this is just not so. These particular crankshafts are all very old now, most having had a lot of hard use in the last thirty years, or so. They're also prone to cracking, especially if they have been used in competition at some stage. **Caution!** - there is no real substitute for the late model large journal crankshaft as found in all A+ 1275cc engines.

A duplex (twin row) timing chain and sprocket set does need to be fitted in place of the standard simplex (single row) item fitted as standard to all factory specification A-Series engines. The reason for this requirement is that simplex timing chains wear out relatively quickly, even on a standard engine. It's not uncommon for a standard engine which has covered 50,000 miles/80,000 kilometres to have an unbelievably loose and noisy timing chain. The noise is not really the problem, of course, but as a symptom of chain wear indicates that the chain has worn so much that camshaft timing could be anything up to 10 degrees or more retarded, and this definitely is a problem. Simplex timing chains do not tend to break, even in higher performance applications, but they do wear excessively. Given the cost of an aftermarket duplex timing chain and sprockets, which will hold the camshaft timing setting five times as long as a simplex chain, there is really no point in fitting a new simplex chain on the basis of maintaining the specified camshaft timing long term.

If a new simplex chain has to be fitted on the basis of cost and/or availability, be aware that it should be replaced every 25,000 miles/40,000 kilometres to ensure that the camshaft timing is not getting too retarded. In this situation always use a genuine Austin/Rover simplex timing chain and not an equivalent replacement part (they seldom seem to be as good).

An engine based on the A+ 1275cc unit can, with the addition of certain bolt-on parts, give a quite remarkable performance for a considerable period of time provided revs are not taken too high. 7000rpm is the reasonable limit for one of these engines (there seldom being a situation where 7000rpm is not enough for road going applications. Up to 7000rpm these engines can be considered near 'bullet proof' (occasional failures excepted).

Changing the clutch plate and timing chain are simple jobs with the engine out of the car and can be carried out with some difficulty with the engine in place.

1098CC

The next best engine after the 1275 is the 1098cc. It's the best of the small bore engines for road use because it has the longest stroke of all A-Series units (making it very torquey for its capacity). This engine, suitably prepared, will pull from 1500rpm in top gear on flat roads without any difficulty and will pull strongly from 2000rpm through to 6000rpm. These engines have plenty of torque and produce it over a wide rev band. They'll 'pull' a high ratio (2.9, 3.1 or 3.2) final drive-equipped standard ratio gearbox very well and, suitably prepared, can deliver excellent fuel economy. The hillclimbing ability of these engines in a Mini, modified and tuned as described in this book is very, very good.

Caution! - Avoid revving a standard component 1098cc engine above 6000rpm. They're generally fine up to this rpm, but there's a definite risk of bottom end failure at higher revs. These engines have the weakest crankshaft/connecting rod combination of any A-Series. 6000rpm on a road going engine is not bad and reliability is virtually guaranteed up to this rev limit.

In view of the potential bottom end problem with 1098cc units, the main and big end bearings should always be replaced when a high mileage engine (50,000 miles/80,000 kilometres) is going to be used as the basis for a high performance unit. Once the bearing shells become worn, the load carrying capacity of the bearing reduces and the crankshaft is then no longer supported as it should be. Failure is likely in this situation.

The other aspect of this situation is that after 75,000 to 100,000 miles/120,000-160,000km, the centre main journal will almost certainly no longer be perfectly round. It will most likely be oval; often by as much as 0.002in/0.05mm or more. In fact, it's likely that the centre main crankshaft journal will be in a worse state than the pair of main bearings it was 'running' in. This is purely to do with the 'whip' or 'skipping rope' effect of the crankshaft due to the fact that it's not very rigid. The solution to this problem is to have the main bearing journals of the crankshaft reground 0.010in/undersize. This will restore the situation for another 60,000miles/100,000km at the very least.

When BMC made the 1098cc MG Midget and Austin Healey Sprite versions of this engine, it was well aware of the problem, and the crankshaft main bearing diameters were increased by 1/4in/0.250in/6.3mm to increase the overlap of the journals (journal overlap being the factor that determines the rigidity of a crankshaft). The main bearing's journal diameters were then 2in, compared to 1 3/4in. Doing this increased the overall rigidity of the crankshaft as well as increasing the main bearing surface area. This was the solution to the crankshaft 'whip' problem up to about 6500rpm on these engines. The main caps in these MG Midget engines were also secured by studs and nuts, rather than bolts!

The oil pump should always be replaced with a new unit when one of these engines has covered a large mileage (more than 50,000 miles/80,000 kilometres). As standard these engines have pin drive oil pumps and the oil pump spindle tangs have been known to break off after the engine has covered high mileages. The engine is usually ruined as a result. The fitting of a brand new oil pump is the very least that should be done. The best thing to do is to replace the camshaft and oil pump with slot drive A+-types, but this does involve some reworking of the block. The block has to have a couple of holes drilled and tapped to bolt in the later model oil pump and an aftermarket aluminium spacer must be fitted between the oil pump and the block. This modification

15

is still more or less a 'bolt-in' exercise, resulting in a much more reliable oil pump drive system (this same recommendation applies to the early non A+ 998cc engine).

An oil pump change can, of course, only be made with the engine out of the car and the engine separated from the gearbox (this is a considerable amount of work). Serious 1098cc engine devotees will often go to the trouble of doing this just to make sure that the engine is as reliable as possible.

998cc A+

The next engine to consider is the 998cc. This is the most common of the small bore engines and it's readily available because it was used in the Metro: it was made A+ from 1980 on. There are thousands of these engines around at give away prices (in the UK at least) which can give good power with very good economy, but they're frequently replaced by 1275cc units for the power improvement offered by this straightforward swap.

If your car is fitted with a 998cc engine in very good condition and you're looking for a reasonable increase in power, but don't want to lose too much economy, this engine can deliver the goods. Substituting a few parts here and there at weekends, and so on, can make the A+ 998cc engine an excellent unit. It is one of the most reliable A-Series engines and responds well to mild tuning via substitute parts and a good tune up.

OTHER CAPACITIES

There have been many A-Series engine sizes over the years, but the three engine sizes mentioned already are by far the most common and widely used today. All three can power a Mini very well. Everyone seems to have a favourite engine size. Anyone who spends the time and money on any of the less common engine sizes (850cc, for example) is doing so for a reason other than wanting power at the most economical cost. There is nothing wrong with wanting to do up an 850cc engine for your Mini. They are good engines, although they're getting a bit hard to find these days. All A-Series engines can be made to go well, and all A-Series engines respond to the same sort of treatment.

Chapter 3

Which cylinder head?

For road use there are some standard production cylinder heads that are better than others. The best flowing readily available volume production cylinder heads are the large inlet valve (1.406in/35.7mm) A+ ones as found on 1300 (1275cc) MG Metro engines. These cylinder heads were, however, never fitted with hardened exhaust valve seats by the factory. The reason being that the factory engineers didn't think there was enough room to fit a good-sized valve seat insert while maintaining these valve sizes.

Cylinder heads which were factory-fitted with hardened valves seats were those made from 1989 and on, which, of course, limits them to 998cc and 1275cc engines. The large inlet valve MG Metro type cylinder head was discontinued in 1989, and only the smaller inlet valve, or standard 1275cc valve sized cylinder heads were available. These cylinder heads were able to take a good-sized hardened exhaust valve seat and they remained

the only cylinder head available until 1275 A-Series engine production ceased.

All 998cc engine cylinder heads made from 1989 on were factory-fitted with hardened inlet and exhaust valve seats and, like their 1275 counterparts, can take unleaded fuel without the need for an additive. The hardened exhaust valve seats used in both heads are pretty much indestructible and, unless the cylinder head distorts, they will never need to be reground/remachined.

Caution! - If any A-Series cylinder head you have or find is cracked do not be tempted to have it repaired. Cut your losses, scrap it and find another which is crack free. Provided the casting is in good condition (no cracks) there isn't any part of the head that can't be replaced or remachined by an engine reconditioner/machine shop. Even terminally damaged exhaust valve seats can be repaired by fitting hardened valve seat inserts.

All of the heads covered in the following text can be simply 'bolted-on' (reconditioning work excepted) which is more or less a few hours fitting work. The machining work and general refurbishment suggested is nothing more than making sure that the cylinder head is efficient and will give reliable service. It would be unreasonable to expect not to have to restore valve seats and skim heads after the miles that most second-hand units have done by this time. Many of the cylinder heads available are 30 to 35 years old and few are less than 10 to 15 years old. The fitting of hardened exhaust valve seats is usually desirable as it modernises the engine.

Because of the age of all A-Series engines, especially engines found in scrapyards, the cylinder head must be skimmed (lightly planed) to clean it up to avoid early cylinder head gasket failure. Engine reconditoners/machine shops resurface cylinder heads all day every day. Consider it mandatory to

The depth of a standard cylinder head is approximately 2.750in/69.9mm.

have the cylinder head skimmed just to be sure that it is dead flat (0.005in/0.125mm to 0.010in/0.250mm to come off the cylinder head).

A-Series cylinder heads are, on average, factory machined to 2.750in/69.8mm thickness. If any cylinder head you find is thinner than this the cylinder head has usually already had the gasket surface planed and this may well limit the head's suitability (eg: if

a head planed by 0.060in/1.5mm is fitted to a 998cc engine with flat-top pistons, for example, the compression ratio could be too high for the octane rating of the fuel available). Use a vernier calliper to check cylinder head thickness.

1275CC ENGINES
All 1275cc engine cylinder head combustion chambers have a volume

Standard MG Metro 1300 cylinder head's combustion chamber and valves.

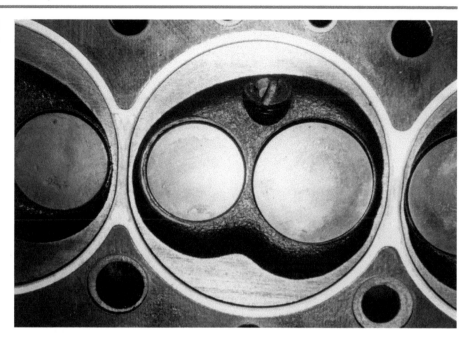

of 21.5cc as standard. Changing the compression ratios (CRs) on some later engines was achieved by varying the distance between the crown of the piston and the top of the bore at top dead centre (TDC). A standard 1275cc engine's cylinder head is between 2.725in/69.3mm to 2.750in/63.9mm in thickness, with most being 2.725in/69.3mm thick.

1300 MG Metro, 1275 Metro Sport and Vanden Plas leaded fuel heads (pre 1989)

The 1300 MG Metro, 1275 Metro Sport and Vanden Plas cylinder heads (the same heads) are the very best of the standard original equipment cylinder heads and should be the first choice for use with any 1275cc A-Series engine intended for high performance road use. These cylinder heads were well finished at the factory so don't require further work and can be fitted to any 1275cc engine as a straight swap for the original head.

The 1300 MG Metro cylinder heads are large inlet-valved cylinder heads with good sized inlet ports which are large enough for any road going 1275cc engine. As far as factory made readily available cylinder heads that can be bought very cheaply are concerned, it simply doesn't get any better than this. These cylinder heads used to be reasonably readily available from scrapyards in the UK, but the day of the Metro is largely over now, and most have disappeared from the roads. These cylinder heads are now getting hard to get. The inlet valves The inlet valves are 1.406in/35.7mm diameter and the exhausts 1.150in/29.2mm diameter.

These cylinder heads were painted red by the factory when they were made. 1300 MG Metro cylinder heads are very well finished compared with other 1275cc A-Series heads. The only problem in using these heads today is that they are not particularly suitable for hardened valve seat conversion (not enough 'meat' in the cylinder head around the exhaust valve and specifically between the inlet valve seat and the exhaust valve seat). Today, a

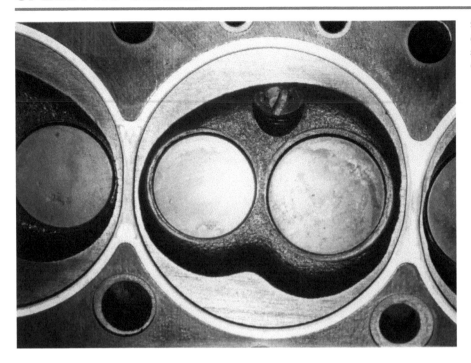

Standard MG Metro Turbo cylinder head combustion chamber and valves. The standard 1275cc engine's combustion chamber is almost exactly the same shape.

lead substitute additive will have to be used if one of these cylinder heads is going to be used.

1300 MG Metro Turbo head

The next best readily available cylinder head is the 1300 MG Metro Turbo unit, but it has smaller inlet valves than the straight 1300 MG Metro cylinder head. Nevertheless, it's still a very good cylinder head for any 1275cc engine though more restrictive than the non-turbo 1300 MG Metro cylinder head because of its smaller inlet valves. In the final analysis, inlet valve size is not all that critical for road use and you'll be very hard pressed to tell the difference between the Turbo and non-Turbo heads in practice.

Despite its smaller valve head size, the Turbo head inlet ports are, on average, the largest of any production A-Series engine ever made. The inlet valves are 1.312in/33.3mm diameter and the exhausts 1.150in/29.2mm.

1300 MG Metro Turbo cylinder heads are well finished, compared with the standard 1275cc A-Series cylinder heads, and can be fitted with hardened valve seats. They are not, however, as well finished as 1300 MG Metro cylinder heads. In fact, it's this type of cylinder head which was fitted with hardened exhaust valve seats by the factory from 1989 on.

These later cylinder heads are the ones today.

Cooper 'S' heads

Next in the desirability stakes we have 1275cc Cooper 'S' heads, but they're not as readily available and were never made in the same numbers as the large inlet valve Metro 1275cc units.

There have also been three basic Cooper S cylinder heads: MkI, MkII and MkIII. Of the three, the MkIII is the best on the basis of reliability. The MkI and MkII cylinder heads had the largest exhaust valve head diameters (1.214in/ 31mm) ever fitted by the factory and, consequently, tend to crack between the inlet and exhaust valve seats. The MkIII cylinder head with its smaller

The standard 850cc/998cc engines' combustion chambers looked like this, and remained this shape for the entire production run of small bore A-series engines as fitted to Minis (1959-1992).

exhaust valve heads (1.150in/29.2mm) did not crack in service. The MkIII cylinder head was very well finished by the factory.

Note that Cooper S cylinder heads have two extra head studs (11 stud holes in all) whereas the MG Metro cylinder heads don't (9 stud holes). It's quite acceptable to fit a Cooper S cylinder head onto any 9 stud block: just ignore the redundant holes.

These Cooper S cylinder heads are not all that easy to come by, but they're still available if you look for them especially at autojumbles and swap meets. If the casting is crack free and does not have grossly sunken or damaged valve seats, it can be restored to as good as new by an engine reconditioner/machine shop.

The large (1.406in/35.7mm) inlet valve cylinder heads such as Cooper 'S,' 1300 MG Metro and pre-1989 Vanden Plas and Metro Sport units, for example, are not really suitable for the fitting of hardened valve seat inserts to

allow their use with unleaded fuel.

850CC, 998CC AND 1098CC ENGINES

These engine's cylinder heads can be planed to increase the compression ratio by a reasonable amount, certainly enough for road use. **Caution!** - The general CR limit for road use with today's 95 RON octane unleaded fuel is 8.9:1 - 9.3:1; with 97 RON octane unleaded fuel the CR to use is 9.3:1 to 10:1; and with today's 98.3 RON octane Shell Optimax, consider 10.3:1 to be about the limit (this RON octane requirement applies to 1275cc engines as well).

All 850cc, 998cc and 1098cc heads can be planed 0.080in/2.0mm from the original thickness of 2.750in/ 69.3mm. Use this as the base original size from which the final minimum thickness of 2.670in/67.8mm or anywhere in between can be used without oil/waterway breakthrough complications of any sort.

'295' casting number cylinder head.

'295' combustion chamber in close up.

850cc, 998cc and 1098cc standard head

The standard 850cc/998cc cylinder head with its 24.5cc combustion chamber volume has small inlet and exhaust valves (1.098in/27.9mm inlet, 1.005in/25.5mm exhaust) and is regarded as the least desirable cylinder head to have on a 998cc engine.

These heads have round inlet

The number '295' is cast into the middle of the cylinder head adjacent to where the rocker shaft bolts on.

The inlet valve on the left has been back chamfered with a 30 degree cut to narrow the seat down as has the exhaust valve on the right. Seat widths after chamfering are 0.040inch/1.0mm for the inlets and 0.070inch/1.8mm for the exhausts. The valve seats in the cylinder head are machined to match.

ports at about 3/4in/20mm in from the side of the cylinder head to which the inlet manifold bolts. The inlet ports are also bored to a specific diameter (0.950in/24mm) in the interests of gaining maximum economy from the engine. Open this hole size up and the economy will never be the same again, even at part throttle. ALL other A-Series cylinder heads have as cast, 'squarish' inlet ports with some more 'squarish' than others and there is a range of inlet port sizes (height and width dimensions).

The 1098cc engine has a similar looking combustion chamber which has a slightly larger inlet valve (1.156in/29.3mm) but has the same size exhaust valves as the 850cc/998cc unit and 26.1cc combustion chamber volume.

Neither of these cylinder heads has much of a performance image but, before discarding them, be aware that they can both be planed by up to 0.080 inch/2.0mm and can be given 0.040in/1.0mm wide inlet valve seats and 0.070in/1.8mm wide exhaust valve seats. These simple modifications will offer a worthwhile performance improvement at very reasonable cost. These cylinder heads are not inefficient, it's just that they were designed to give reasonable engine performance with maximum economy.

'295' casting number heads
One frequently mentioned cylinder head for use on 998cc and 1098cc engines (the same head) is the '295' casting number head found on 998cc Cooper, MG 1100, Wolseley 1100 and 1098cc MG Midget/Austin Healey Sprite. The problem is usually finding one of these heads in good condition, but they're around if you look at autojumble sales or swapmeets.

The one thing that all 998cc and 1098cc cylinder heads, including the '295' have in common is that their combustion chambers overlap the bores by a considerable amount on the exhaust valve side. Nevertheless, when using these cylinder heads the standard 1.0in/25.4mm exhaust valve cannot come into contact with the top of the cylinder block under any

circumstances. It's true there's not a lot of clearance between the valve and the side of the bore, but there is some. In fact, the seated exhaust valve heads are approximately 0.400-0.425inch/10.0-10.7mm below the head gasket surface of the cylinder head. As a consequence, with just 0.318in/8.0mm of valve lift there's no possibility of an exhaust valve coming anywhere near the block. Even if these cylinder heads are planed by 0.080in/2.0mm, which is the maximum recommended, the inlet and exhaust valve heads do not protrude above the gasket surface of the cylinder head, let alone come near the block deck.

Provided a '295'-type cylinder head is crack free, has reground inlet valves, reground inlet and exhaust valve seats, new exhaust valves, all new valve guides or K-lined originals and has been skimmed to ensure that the cylinder head gasket face is flat (or skimmed further to increase compression), it will deliver good fuel economy and very acceptable engine power on the road.

The problem with these cylinder heads is that they have very large combustion chamber volume (28.2cc) as they were designed to run with flat-topped pistons and the compression will be very low if fitted to a 998cc/1098cc engine which has dish-topped pistons. '295' heads can be planed 0.080in/2.0mm maximum to reduce combustion chamber volume to approximately 23.5cc (and therefore increase compression) but they still won't match a standard 1275cc cylinder head which has a smaller combustion chamber volume (21.5cc) and larger valves just as it comes from the factory.

The '295' head was very well finished at the factory and is fine for a flat-topped piston 998cc or 1098cc engine. The inlet ports though

smallish are a decent size and, as a consequence, reasonable fuel economy is assured.

'295' head planing of 0.080in/2.0mm will reduce combustion chamber volume from 28.2cc to approximately 23.5cc and will increase CR from 9.3:1 to 9.6:1 on a 998cc engine or from 8.9:1 to 10.2:1 on a 1098cc flat-top piston engine.

As there is plenty of material around the exhaust valve seat, '295' heads can be fitted with hardened valve seats by an engine reconditioner/machine shop to allow the use of unleaded fuel. This is a worthwhile modification for long term reliability.

Fitting a '295' casting cylinder head onto ANY small bore engine is the best option on the basis of good all round engine performance with economy. BMC engineers knew what they were doing when they made these cylinder heads; they really are excellent heads.

'295' head on 850cc engine
A '295' casting number cylinder head planed by 0.080inch/2.0mm (from original standard dimensions) can be easily fitted to a standard 8.3:1 compression ratio 850cc engine. CR will rise to 8.8:1 and this, together with this head's better cylinder filling, will result in a much better performing engine.

Note. The reason these small bore A-Series engines' cylinder heads can only be planed a maximum of 0.080in from standard is due to the close proximity of the oil-way drilling to the gasket surface. 1275cc engine cylinder heads have the oil-way drilling positioned higher up in the cylinder head casting, and are not limited by this factor. The limiting factor on a 1275cc cylinder head is the spark plug holes on the combustion chamber side.

Having the top of the block

planed to bring the tops of the pistons flush with the block deck will result in a further useful increase in compression ratio and further increased performance. This does of course mean removing the engine and gearbox from the car and then removing the engine from the gearbox, though the engine does not have to be stripped to do this as the cylinder bores can be carefully masked off. The block will need to be planed by about 0.020inch/0.5mm and then cleaned thoroughly after machining. After block planing CR will be approximately 9.2:1 which will give better performance, but there's quite a lot of work involved.

1275CC CYLINDER HEADS ON 850CC, 998CC AND 1098CC ENGINES

Small bore engine '295' casting number heads are becoming rare. However, given that most 850cc, 998cc and 1098cc engines are fitted with dish-top pistons (low CR, even if used with a maximum planed '295' casting cylinder head), one alternative would be to fit a standard 1275cc engine's cylinder head.

All of these 1275cc cylinder heads are much better flowing at the expense of some fuel economy than the standard 850cc and 998cc heads and give increased CR as standard because of their reduced combustion chamber volume. The inlet ports are quite large, but not too large, for a 998cc and 1098cc engine. They are, however, a little bit too large for the 850cc engine, but this is still a good alternative, especially the cylinder head from the standard production 1275cc engine.

However, there are a few points which do need to be checked if this is to be a straightforward and uncomplicated swap.

Usually standard 998cc engines have 8.3:1 CR and 1098cc engines

8.5:1 CR (dished-topped pistons in both cases). Fitting a 1275cc engine head results in an approximate increase in compression of 9.0:1 for the 998cc engine and 9.4:1 for the 1098cc unit. The CR increases because the volume of the combustion chambers is smaller (21.5cc) in the replacement head. Note that for use with 95 octane fuel, CRs of 9.0:1 and 9.4:1 are still to low to be ideal for best all round engine performance.

A 1275cc engine cylinder head gasket **must** be used when fitting a 1275cc head to a smaller capacity engine as there are waterway alignment problems when the standard 998cc or 1098cc gasket is used with a 1275cc head.

Caution! - It must be clearly understood that when fitting 1275cc cylinder heads to 850cc, 998cc or 1098cc blocks the exhaust valve will hit the top of the block if there is not enough clearance for the valve head. This happens for three reasons. First, the exhaust valve heads are larger in diameter (1.150in/29.2mm, compared to 1.000in/25.4mm). Secondly, the valve guide centres are wider spaced. Thirdly, the combustion chambers are much shallower, meaning that the amount of valve lift provided by the camshaft plays a significant part in how close the heads of the valves come to the top of the block.

The most significant factor here - and the only one that really needs to be considered - is valve lift and, if the cylinder head is planed, how much clearance there will be between the head of the valve and the block deck at full valve lift when the engine is assembled and running.

For standard non A+ 998cc or 1098cc engines (fitted with standard camshafts which have relatively little exhaust valve lift of 0.285in/7.2mm), for example, 1275cc heads (with

inlet and exhaust valve seats re-cut to restore them to original condition) can usually be planed by 0.035in/ 0.9mm. This amount of planing usefully increases CR, usually without causing exhaust valve to block deck interference.

There's no doubt that these engines go better with 10:1 through 10.3:1 CR, as opposed to 9.3:1 with 97 octane unleaded or 98.3 RON Shell Optimax fuel, which means that the cylinder head or the top of the block, or both, need to be planed to reduce the volume of the combustion area.

The only potential problem with the 1275cc head conversion is that the exhaust valves can come into contact with the top of the block if the head has been planed. In most instances there's sufficient clearance and, what's more, extra clearance is obtained when the valve seats are reground (sinking them further into the head) to clean them up. Through valve seat regrinding an extra, and possibly vital, 0.010-0.015in/0.25-0.40mm can be obtained. A further 0.020inch/0.5mm of clearance can be obtained by fitting slimline-headed racing exhaust valves which are not expensive and are made of top quality material. If new valves are going to be bought anyway, the small extra cost of racing valves is well worthwhile because the cylinder head can be planed an extra 0.020inch/0.5mm providing even more compression.

With the use of slimline racing exhaust valves coupled with reseating the exhaust valves into the cylinder head, it's quite possible to gain an extra 0.030-0.040inch./0.75-1.0mm exhaust valve head to block deck clearance over the standard cylinder head (hardened exhaust valve seat cylinder heads excepted).

If, at this point, the engine block is not attached to the gearbox, consider

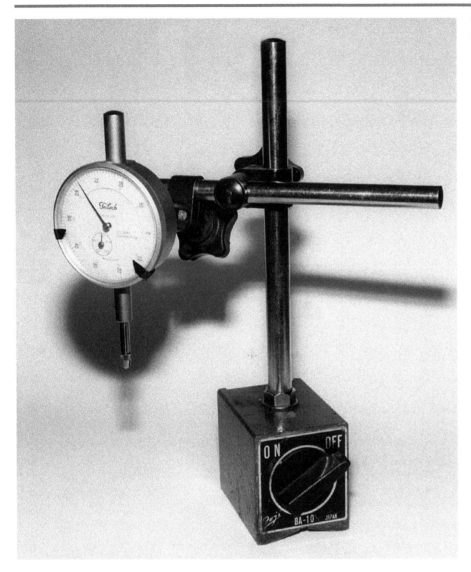

Typical dial test indicator (dial gauge) and magnetic stand.

having the block deck planed so that the piston crowns are bought up flush with the top of the block (usually 0.020inch/0.5mm needs to be removed). This modification does not really fit this book's 'bolt-on' criteria, however, if the engine is not in the car it is certainly worth considering. Block planing in conjunction with a planed 1275cc head will get the CR of an 8.3:1 998cc engine up to 10.0:1 and an 8.5:1 1098cc up to or 10.3:1.

Cutting pockets into the block deck would clearly obviate all potential for valve to block clearance and offer scope for deeper planing, but the procedure is beyond the scope of this book. For those who would like information on this modification there is another specialist book in the Veloce SpeedPro range: *How To Power Tune The BMC/BL/Rover 998 A-Series Engine* by Des Hammill. Note that while this book is 998cc engine specific, the pocketing information can be applied equally to 850cc and 1098cc engine blocks. With an appropriately pocketed block any valve

Valve is at full lift. Zero the dial and then count back as the valve returns to its seat.

These cylinder heads are not as well machined as the earlier Cooper 'S' or A+ MG Metro heads. The inlet ports are also smaller than the Cooper 'S' or A+ 1300 MG/Vanden Plas ones, but this gives good fuel economy without significantly affecting engine performance 'on the road'. The other factor is that the combustion chamber, while not being particularly 'neat' is slightly deeper and this adds up to more exhaust valve head to block clearance. In many instances the standard 1275cc cylinder head can be planed 0.040in/1.0mm without valve head to block deck clearance problems. Check the original dimensions before planing any of these cylinder heads: this way not too much material will be removed from the head gasket face of the cylinder head.

The problem with most of the better readily available production cylinder heads (MG Metro) is that the inlet ports are actually a little bit large if one of these cylinder head is put on a smaller capacity engine such as an 850cc, 998cc or 1098cc. An MG head is not the way to maximum economy even though a good power

lift and any amount of cylinder head planing can be accommodated.

You can use any standard 1275cc Mini pre-A+ engine's head or the 1275cc Metro 1300 (non-MG/Vanden Plas) A+ engine's cylinder head on a 850cc, 998cc or 1098cc engine.

With the cylinder head assembled, the distance from the cylinder head matching surface down to the flat surface of the exhaust valve head is measured using the tail of a vernier calliper. Measure each exhaust valve: the smallest dimension is the one to use for calculations. Include the compressed head gasket thickness in the full amount of clearance.

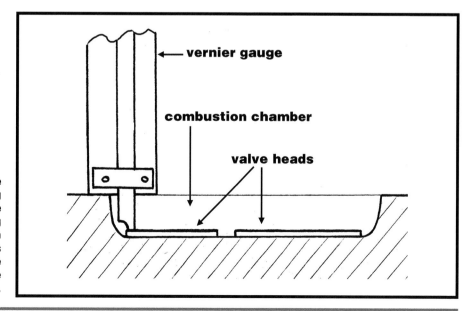

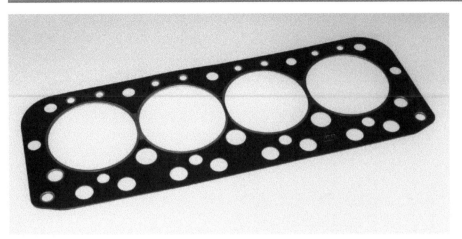

Unipart Metro Turbo cylinder head gasket.

increase will result. For best economy the standard 1275cc engine's cylinder head is the head to use.

Measuring exhaust valve to deck clearance

Within the range of engines covered by this book, the theoretical greatest exhaust valve lift with a standard camshaft is 0.318in/8.0mm (1300 MG Metro) while the least is 0.285in/7.24mm. In reality, few valves seem to make the specified amount of lift, many achieving 0.010-0.020in/0.25-0.5mm less. **Caution!** - If you're planning to use a different cylinder head (1275cc) on your 850cc, 998cc or 1098cc engine you must measure what exhaust valve lift the camshaft you have in your engine gives. This is easy enough to do when the engine is assembled before the original cylinder head is removed from the engine and only takes 20 to 30 minutes.

Remove the sparkplugs and the rocker cover and set the exhaust valve clearance to what is recommended (0.012in/0.3mm for a standard camshaft). Next, with the tail of a vernier calliper measure the distance from the top of the valve retainer to the cylinder head casting (or, if the tail of the vernier calliper is small enough, the 'spot facing' (machined platform) of the valve spring platform). Now turn the engine over by hand until you see tha valve reach full lift (spring at maximum compression). With the valve at full lift take a second measurement of the distance from the top of the valve spring retainer to the cylinder head casting (or valve spring platform). Subtract the full lift measurement from the first measurement taken and the result is the actual valve lift of the particular valve. Repeat the full process to check the figure. Carry out the same measuring procedure on the remaining three exhaust valves. Expect the valve lift measurements of all the valves to be quite similar (but not necessarily to the manufacturer's specified height). If one measurement is much less than the others, suspect that the camshaft lobe operating that valve is worn (camshaft will need replacement).

A precise method of measuring valve lift is the use of a dial indicator (dial gauge). All engine reconditioners/machine shops have this sort of equipment. The instrument's magnetic stand clamps onto the cylinder head (rocker cover gasket surface) and the dial indicator needle is positioned on the valve retainer so that maximum lift can be measured to 0.001in/0.025mm

When new, most 1300 MG

Metro and 1275 Sport cylinder heads had the heads of the exhaust valves 0.280-0.290in/7.1-7.4mm below the cylinder head matching (gasket) surface. In most instances, after recutting the valve seats to clean them up, the distance will end up between 0.295-0.310in/7.5-7.9mm. To this figure can be added the thickness of the cylinder head gasket (never less than 0.035in/0.79mm and seldom more than 0.050in/1.2mm).

This means, as an example, that with the thinnest cylinder head gasket available which is 0.035 inches when compressed, plus, say, 0.300inch/7.6mm (measured distance between valve head and cylinder head gasket surface) there is a total amount of valve movement possible of 0.335in/8.5mm. Deduct this from the actual exhaust valve lift and the valve head to block deck clearance can be easily calculated (do the measurements for each valve). The cylinder head can then be planed by an amount that allows 0.020in/0.5mm exhaust valve head to block clearance at full valve lift. If you wish, use slimline racing valves to allow extra planing.

The average standard cylinder head gasket is approximately 0.050in/1.25mm thick when new and uncompressed, but is likely to be 0.042-0.045in/0.56-0.64mm thick when the cylinder head has been torqued down. Better quality cylinder head gaskets are likely to compress to 0.035-0.038in/0.89-0.97mm from an uncompressed thickness of 0.040in/1.0mm.

Caution! What can happen with only 0.020in/0.5mm of valve head to block clearance at full valve lift is that if the engine is revved too high the valves can 'bounce' and the block will be contacted by the exhaust valves. This problem can be avoided if the engine is not revved too high and the

valve springs are of sufficient tension to allow 6300-6500rpm capability. New 1300 MG Metro single spring and 1300 MG Metro Turbo double valve springs are capable of the required level of valve control. These valve springs are available new from Austin/Rover dealers or A-Series specialists. Having too little valve head to block clearance (less than 0.020in/0.50mm) is not advisable.

Summary
All standard 850cc/998cc and 1098cc engines can be fitted with any 1275cc engine's cylinder head in conjunction with a standard thickness replacement cylinder head gasket. This will reduce the combustion chamber volume from 24.5cc for the 850cc and 998cc engines, and from 26.1cc for the 1098cc engine, to 21.4cc, and increase the compression ratio of all these engines. For best results the inlet and exhaust valve seats need to be re-cut, the inlet and exhaust valves reground and back chamfered. The cylinder head should, at the very least, be 'skimmed' by 0.004in/0.1mm to prevent gasket blowing problems.

Caution! - Once the replacement head is in place, the crankshaft should be rotated by hand (sparkplugs out) for two full revolutions to ensure there are no valve contact (with the block deck) problems. Additionally, each exhaust valve must be positioned at full valve lift and then pushed further open to check that there is clearance between the head of the valve and the block deck. The exhaust valve can be pushed further open by levering the valve retainer. Anyone with reasonable strength can move the valve using two large identically-sized screwdrivers positioned either side of the rocker arm tip and on the valve spring retainer. Further movement, indicating clearance, will be felt by the person

pushing the valve down. This method is a bit crude, but will determine that there is some clearance available.

AFTERMARKET MODIFIED CYLINDER HEADS (ALL ENGINES)
There is an alternative to using standard heads and that is to buy a cylinder head prepared by one of the many very good companies which specialise in this sort of work. The cost of a reworked cylinder head is not really outrageous (although it may seem so compared to that of a cylinder head from a scrapyard) and these heads are 'bolt-on.'

Most companies which modify A-Series cylinder heads fit new valves, guides, valve springs, collets, retainers and often offer hardened valve seats as an extra so that unleaded fuel can be used. These cylinder heads can represent excellent value for money when the value of this complete refurbishment, as well as the porting, is taken into account.

The other angle on this is if a good second-hand (but properly modified) cylinder head is purchased at a very reasonable price. Bargains can be found, of course, and so can 'lemons.' It's amazing what some vendors will pass off, or try and pass off, as being good. There are risks attached to buying from autojumbles/swapmeets because when a quick decision has to be made important factors get overlooked. Factors like cracked valve seats, cracked head, burnt valves, worn valve stems and valve guides. Nevertheless, with due care simply excellent cylinder heads can be found for unbelievably reasonable prices and it's for this reason that mention of them is made here, especially small inlet port versions.

Some cylinder head porting concerns offer modified small valve, small bore cylinder heads (a cylinder head that was originally a standard cylinder head on a 998cc or 1098cc engine) for small bore engines. Cylinder heads like this are 'bolt-on' items and give good all round engine performance because they offer increased compression and better gasflow over a standard cylinder head. The increased CR is usually at a moderate level and ports are not too large for decent fuel economy. Generally, such heads are ported so that the internal passageways of the cylinder head are not enlarged all that much, but are smooth in contour. This moderate specification is hard to beat for any small bore engine.

Be aware though that some of these cylinder heads have inlet ports and passageways which are really far too large for road going engines and fuel economy will never be any good (no matter how slowly the car is driven). This disadvantage can be mighty frustrating when the performance benefits of the head can rarely be used on the road. This is the downside of having a racing head or a heavily modified cylinder head on a road going engine. The factory did not make the inlet ports the size they did for nothing!

When a heavily modified head with large inlet ports more suitable for racing is fitted to a road going engine, the economy loss can be dramatic - and for no appreciable gain in power. For example, if a standard 1098cc Mini Clubman engine is fitted with a well modified MG Metro 1300 cylinder head, overall fuel economy will be around 20 to 25 miles to the Imperial gallon in general driving conditions, even with a standard type camshaft fitted to the engine. Change the cylinder head for a standard MkIII Mini Cooper 'S' unit, for example, and the economy improves to about 30 to 35 miles to the Imperial gallon. Change the cylinder head for a standard 1275cc unit planed to give at least 10:1 compression and the economy improves to about 35 to 45 miles to the gallon.

If you want to retain good miles to the gallon don't use a cylinder head with fully opened out inlet ports. Also be aware that many large exhaust valve racing-type 1275 cylinder heads

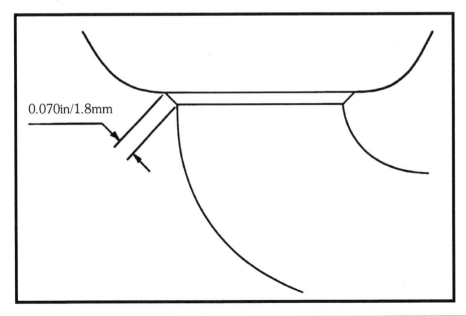

0.070in/1.8mm

The width of the exhaust valve seat as cut in the head is 0.070in/1.8mm, as is the seat width of the actual valve. These two contact areas must match each other perfectly to obtain this width.

All inlet valves must have seat contact areas that look like this and of are the correct width. A very wide valve seat reduces air flow. Three angle inlet valve seats are vital on an A-Series cylinder head. Three angle valve seating is the easy method of simulating the characteristics of a radiused seat.

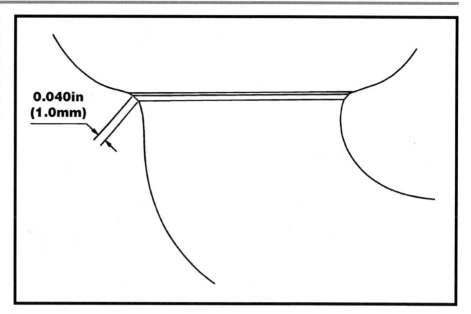

0.040in (1.0mm)

are planed considerably and will not 'bolt-on' fit to a small bore engine (insufficient valve head to block deck clearance).

VALVE SEATS

What makes a difference to any A-Series cylinder head is making sure that the valve seats are in perfect

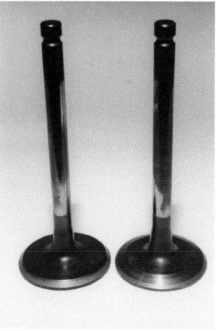

Standard 1.401in/35.6mm inlet valve on the left and a 30 degree back-chamfered standard valve on the right.

condition. Most engines will have covered some miles by now and - with some exceptions - are almost always in need of exhaust valve seat and exhaust valve refurbishment.

Caution! - It's advisable to replace the exhaust valves on any high mileage engine (75,000 miles/120,000km plus) as a preventative measure against valve failure (valve head 'falling off' or burning). With the use of unleaded heads and unleaded fuel on these engines, the valves become the weak link, and they invariably burn out now as opposed to the valve seats. Hardened valve seats are near indestructible but the valves are not!

Exhaust valve seats

The exhaust valve seats have always left something to be desired, especially the two inner ones. Ask the reconditioner who is doing the reseating work for you to make sure that the exhaust valves are sunk into the head an equal amount if possible. The only time this won't be possible is if one seat is badly burned and needs to be sunk further than others to clean it up.

Close-up of back-chamfered standard (1.401in/35.6mm) inlet valve.

The exception to the exhaust valve seat burning problem is the later A+ 998cc engine and small inlet valve (1.3in diameter) are the later A+ 998cc and A+ 1275cc engines made from 1989 on which have hardened exhaust valve seats so that the engines can run on unleaded fuel. These factory fitted valve seat inserts are exceptionally hard (68 Rockwell C) and after many thousands of miles will be found to be in as new condition. It's virtually impossible to find them worn through normal wear and tear - and it's almost impossible to regrind them! Hardened exhaust valve seats are THE solution to using unleaded fuel (without additives) in A-Series engines.

A-Series heads have been made of various grades of cast iron over the years, later heads generally being softer than earlier units. This happened because Austin/Rover sourced their raw castings from various foundries and the material specification varied.

Irrespective of this, no as cast, cast iron A-Series cylinder head is going to be reliable long term using straight unleaded fuel. They can, however, be reasonably reliable for a while using unleaded fuel provided the engine does not operate at elevated temperatures. For example, a lot of town driving where the engine is not getting all that hot, or where the engine's water temperature does not go above 70-75 degrees C, is not going to cause valve seat recession as quickly as you might imagine. Ultimate failure is, however, guaranteed.

Exhaust valve seating is straightforward on any A-series cylinder head: a 45 degree cut. Seat widths vary a bit and, provided the seat is clean with no pit marks or other flaws, it'll give good service. The exhaust valve seat as cut into the cylinder head needs to be 0.070in/1.8mm wide for maximum reliability. This will usually mean that the engine reconditioner will have to use a 60 degree 'inner cut' to narrow the valve seat to get this dimension.

Inlet valve seats

Inlet valves and inlet valve seats fare much better than exhausts because they don't have to contend with the same amount of heat. Most inlet valve seats are unbelievably wide: 0125in/3.2mm, or more, being not uncommon. However, to enhance performance, inlet valve seats and the valve's contact seat must be narrowed down so that they are both 0.040in/1.0mm in width in all A-Series heads.

The maximum size of the valve head diameter must also be utilised. This means that if the inlet valve is 1.406in/35.7mm diameter, for example, the outer diameter of the valve seat in the cylinder head must be 1.406in/35.7mm diameter too (no more, no less). This work can be done as part of a standard refurbishing operation and can be carried out by any engine reconditioner/machine-shop.

Narrowing of valve seat widths to the ideal dimensions can be carried out as an additional process during normal seat refurbishment. It will entail machining a 60 degree 'inner cut' on the port side of the valve seat and a 30 degree 'top cut' on the combustion chamber side of the valve seat. The valve itself will need to be back-chamfered in a valve refacing machine set to 30 degrees. These two extra operations are straightforward machining operations for any engine reconditioner/machine-shop for which you'll be charged an appropriate extra amount.

Caution! - The octane rating and the quality of fuel varies around the world. The amounts of CR mentioned in this chapter relate to engines using

95, 97 and 98.3 RON octane fuels as available

in the UK. You may not be able to use the same CRs with the same RON octane ratings of fuel in other parts of the world. In the UK, these amounts of compression should only be used in conjunction with proven full power mixtures. This means having your engine run on a rolling road dyno to full power, the exhaust gases analysed, and the mixture made so rich that the power starts to reduce. For example, a power run may show that an engine develops a maximum power output of 75bhp at 5800rpm, with an exhaust gas analysed mixture of 6% CO. If the engine is run with a 6.3% CO exhaust gas analysed mixture and the power reading is 72bhp, then the mixture is too rich for the particular engine. Conversely, if the engine is set leaner, at, say, 5.7% CO, and the power reading is the same at 72 bhp, the mixture is too lean. Making the mixture richer or leaner either side of this optimum amount causes the power output to reduce. With such an engine running lean, it might well start to 'pink' with the 5.7% CO setting, whereas it wouldn't with the 6.0% CO setting.

All engines have a peak point where they produce maximum power with an optimum mixture strength. It's quickest and often easiest to take the car to a rolling road operator and have it checked in the prescribed manner. Remember, you don't know what the optimum mixture strength is going to be that produces maximum power on your engine until you have it checked rich and lean either side of the mean maximum power output. This is a common sense approach to obtaining the best possible engine performance using proven scientific analysis.

The maximum compression ratio to use on any engine is the one that allows the use of 34-35 degrees of total ignition advance within the confines of the RON octane rating of the fuel you are using in the engine. The higher the compression ratio the better, provided the engine is not on the 'ragged edge' of 'pinking'. The acid test is that the engine must be capable of accelerating under wide-open throttle through the gears without 'pinking'.

Consider the band of maximum power mixture strengths to be 5.4-6.3% CO, or the equivalent in Lambda or air/fuel ratio.

Note that I have use the 'point of maximum power production' as opposed to maximum rpm - there is a difference. 7000rpm is the magic figure on any A-Series engine and most other two valve per cylinder push rod type engines.

If your engine 'pinks' on the compression ratio you are using, either increase the RON octane rating of the fuel being used, or reduce the compression. Don't reduce the spark/ignition advance and increase the air/fuel mixture ratio. Doing do will only result in reduced power output, higher fuel consumption, higher emissions, and greater bore wear due to the excessive fuel mixture constantly 'washing' the oil film off the bores.

VALVES, COLLETS/KEEPERS/ SPLIT LOCKS, VALVE SPRING RETAINERS AND VALVE SPRINGS

There have been seven standard valve retainer and collet/keeper/split lock combinations (from here on referred to as collets) used on A-Series engines. Although swapping keepers and valve spring retainers around is possible in some instances, the way the combinations are listed here is how the manufacturer intended them to be matched.
Note. All A-Series engine collets and

valve spring retainers have 10 degree tapers.

There were two valve stem diameters used over the years - 0.279in/7.12mm and 0.3133in/7.9mm - with the former being the most common. The larger, and much less common, valve stem diameter was used on the sodium-filled exhaust valves as used on the 1275cc MG Metro Turbo engines, and featured triple-groove collets. Furthermore, the valve spring retainers and their matching keepers were a unique combination, and all Turbo engines featured quite strong dual valve springs.

The valves for 850cc, 998cc and 1098cc engines are all the same overall length, approximately 3.425in/88.0mm, whereas the valves for 1275cc engines are approximately 3.575in/90.7mm. However, while it might appear that the range of standard A-Series engines have similar valve train componentry, it's actually anything but simple, and major errors can be made with standard parts by using the wrong valves, collets and valve spring retainers. The following breakdown of the standard componentry as applied to all A-Series engines will put everything into perspective.

SMALL BORE ENGINES
First combinations
The first A-series Mini engines (categorised as small bore engines, with their 850cc, 997cc, 998cc and1098cc engines) used valves which had a square-edged recess groove in the valve stem for the collets. These collets had a circlip which sat around the top of the collets in a round groove that was formed once the valve combination was assembled. These collets are unique to these valves; the inlet and exhaust valve overall

Early small bore engine valves: exhaust valve used on all small bore 850cc, 998cc and 1098cc engines, extreme left (1.000 inch diameter); 850cc and 998cc single carburettor inlet valves, centre left (1.100 inch diameter); 1098cc single carburettor engine inlet valve, centre right (1.150 inch diameter); and twin carburettor 998cc and 1098cc inlet valve, extreme right (1.219 inch diameter). The valve spring retainer, collets and retaining circlip used by all of the above are at the bottom of the photo.

Collets/keepers/split locks: early style ones for 850cc, 998cc and 1098cc engines, extreme left; 1275cc single groove ones (which were later universally used on all engines up until A+ engines came out) centre left. A+ 998cc and 1275cc triple groove ones for standard diameter valve stems, centre right; A+ MG Metro Turbo, triple groove, large diameter valve stems, extreme right.

length was approximately 3.440-3.450in/87.4-87.5mm for all of them. The 848cc, 997cc Cooper (1961-1963), the single and twin carburettor 1098cc engines all used this type of valve, valve spring retainer and collet/circlip arrangement up until 1974.

The valve stem diameter was 0.279in/7.09mm for all small bore engines (1959-1991).

The exhaust valves were exactly the same for all of these engines and they had a 1.000in/25.4mm diameter head. There were, however, three

head sizes of inlet valve. The 848cc engine had 1.095in/27.8mm valve heads, the single carburettor 1098cc and the 997cc Cooper of 1961 had 1.156in/29.4mm valve heads, and the 998cc Cooper and the twin carburettor 1098cc MG, Riley Kestrel, Wolseley and Vanden-Plas had 1.219in/30.9mm valve heads.

There were single and dual valve spring combinations used on these engines. The 848cc had $1^{11}/_{16}$in/42.86mm free standing length single valve springs with 37lb/17kg of seated pressure and 70lb/32kg of over the nose fully open pressure. The 997cc Cooper and the single carburettor 1098cc engines had the $1^{3}/_{4}$ in/44.45mm free standing length valve springs with 55lb/25kg of seated pressure and 90lb/41kg of open pressure. In the late 1960s the 848cc engine used these stronger single valve spring as well.

The 998cc Mini Cooper, the 1098cc MG, Riley Kestrel, Wolseley and Vanden-Plas engines all used dual valve springs which had a free length of $1^{3}/_{4}$in/44.45mm for the outer and $1^{45}/_{64}$in/43.3mm for the inner. The combined seated pressure was 73lb/33kg and the fully open pressure was 118lb/53kg.

The valve spring retainer is the same for all of the above engines and it is easily recognised by the large 30 degree chamfer on the outer edge and a machined in groove on the top face.

The valve spring fitted height of all small bore engines (848cc, 997cc, 998cc and 1098cc engines) is approximately 1.325in/33.5mm and it remained this size from 1959 across the board until the end of A+ 998cc engine production in 1991. The maximum valve lift with standard valve springs is 0.390-0.400in/9.9-10.1mm. The dual valve springs are the strongest and will allow 6500rpm.

Second combinations

The second valve combination for 848cc, 998cc and 1098cc engines had valves which had a single round groove in the valve stem (1974-1981). The collets now used were those from the 1275cc engine and their introduction was a standardisation measure (one collet for all A-series engines).

The valve spring retainer was now different and, while it had a groove machined in the top surface (deeper and wider than the first retainers), it no longer had a 30 degree chamfer on the outer edge, the edge of the retainer now had a very small, 60 degree chamfer machined onto it for half of its depth, making it easy to identify.

The single valve spring had a free standing height of 1³/₄in/44.45mm which was the same as used previously on 1098cc single carburettor engines. There were two inlet valve head diameters of 1.095in/27.8mm (998cc engines) and 1.156in/29.4mm (1098cc engines) and one exhaust valve head diameter of 1.000in/25.4mm for these two engine capacities. The difference between the valves was confined to the collet groove. The large diameter, 1.219in/30.9mm inlet valves were not carried over to these engines, and neither were the dual valve springs. The last 850cc and 1098cc engines were available for part of 1981.

Note that some of the last 1098cc engines had a different valve spring fitted height, and used standard 1275cc single valve springs. They are not included in the general specification because only a very few were made.

Third combination

The third combination for the A+ 998cc engines of 1980-1991 had triple groove collets and valve stems. There were two valve spring retainers used on these engines and both are of

Early 850cc, 998cc and 1098cc groove-top valve spring retainer with chamfered outer edge (left); later 850cc, 998cc and 1098cc groove-top valve spring retainer with small recessed but otherwise square outer edge (centre); and an A+ MG Metro Turbo groove-top valve spring retainer with a square outer edge (right).

identical specification, and each has a raised ridge on the top of the surface around where the two collets fit. One is made of sintered steel (black) and the other is turned from steel bar. The steel retainers have a 30 degree turned chamfer on the outer top edge, while the sintered ones have a 30 degree outer edge and some have a radiused outer top edge. The raised edge on the top surface of these retainers is what categorises them as a type.

Only one size of inlet valve and exhaust valve was used from this point on. The inlet valve head diameter was 1.095in/27.8mm, and the exhaust was 1.000in/25.4mm. The single valve spring used through to the end of production was the same one used on the previous 998cc and 1098cc engines (seated pressure of 55lb/25kg, and an over the nose pressure of 90lb/41kg).

The idea behind the use of triple groove collets was to allow for valve stem rotation while the engine was running, thus promoting better valve seat (cylinder head) and valve wear.

The outer valve springs of all small bore engines are made of 0.140in/4.5mm diameter wire. This is easy to measure with a vernier caliper making positive identification of valve springs

straightforward. The inner valve spring was wound using 0.085in/2.2mm diameter wire.

The single carburettor 850cc and 1098cc engines had a valve lift of 0.285in/7.2mm until they were phased out in 1981, as did the 998cc engines up until this time. The twin carburettor 997cc, 998cc and 1098cc engines had 0.312in/7.8mm of valve lift. The later A+ 998cc engines had 0.312in/7.8mm of valve lift.

The small bore engines as used in Minis and Metros used the pressed steel rocker arms from 1959 to 1978, and the sintered type from 1978-1991. Forged rocker arms were used on all small bore engines but, on A35/Morris Minor types, they are interchangeable.

LARGE BORE ENGINES

With the advent of the 970cc, 1071cc and 1275cc Cooper S engines in 1963, there was a new A-Series engine derivative. The 970cc and 1071cc engines finished in 1964, but the 1275cc Cooper S engine went on to 1971. These large bore 1275cc engines are all very easy to recognise because they have tapper chest plates, all other 1275cc engines don't. In 1970 the standard single carburettor 1275cc engine was introduced on Minis (1275

GT) and continued in various guises until 2001.

These Cooper S engines all came equipped with forged rocker arms (A35/Morris Minor type). All small bore Mini engines and single carburettor 1275cc engines up to 1973 used the pressed steel type rocker arms and from 1973 and on, all A-Series engines were fitted with sintered rocker arms (introduced on the Allegro actually).

All of the 1275cc engines up until the time the engine was made A+ used the single groove collets and retainers that were introduced on the first Cooper S engines. These valve spring retainers are recognisable by the 30 degree outer edge chamfer and 1/16in wide 45 degree chamfer where the collet taper meets the top surface of the retainer. The single groove collets are the same as those used on the small bore engines.

All of the large bore A-series engines cylinder heads have used valves which are 3.570-3,575in/90.6-90.8mm in overall length. The standard valve spring fitted height was also approximately 1.390in/35.3mm. There were two inlet valve head diameters used and two exhaust ones. There were two valve stem diameters (0.279in/7.09mm for inlet and exhaust) which is the same as the small bore engines, with the exception being the exhaust valves used on the A+ MG Metro Turbo engines (1981-1989). These engines had 0.317in/7.96mm diameter exhaust valve stems. This also meant that there were two triple groove collets used on A+ 1275cc engines.

The Cooper S engines (1963-1968 MkIs and 1968-1970 MkIIs) used 1.400in/35.6mm head diameter inlet valves and 1.214in/30.8mm head diameter exhaust valves and single groove valve stems. The exhaust valve head diameter was reduced on the

MkIII Cooper S engines (1970-1971) because of a cylinder head cracking problem (not enough material between the inlet and exhaust valve seats). The exhaust valve head diameter was reduced to 1.156in/29.3mm. That's three Cooper S valves between 1963 and 1971.

The Cooper S engines used dual valve springs which gave a seated pressure of approximately 75lb/34kg and an over the nose pressure of approximately 140lb/64kg at the standard lift of 0.318in/8.1mm. The free length of new outer Cooper S valve spring was 1.750in/44.5mm and the inners were 1.700in/43.2mm. These coil springs in combination were coil bound at approximately 0.965in/24.5mm, which meant that, with a 'coil clearance' of 0.040in/1.0mm, they would allow up to 0.385in/9.5mm of valve lift and at that height an over the nose pressure of approximately 150lb/68kg. This is enough valve spring pressure for a lot of applications (over 6500rpm).

There was another valve spring retainer available in the mid-1960s which was developed by Weslake Laboratories for racing purposes. It is easy to identify by the capital 'W' stamped on the top surface of the retainer. This retainer was made of high tensile steel and had a smaller taper for the collets, thus giving a reduced fitted valve spring height (0.050in/1.25mm less) and increased valve spring pressure with the low camshafts used in those days.

Single carburettor 1275cc engines

The first Mini to have a 1275cc single carburettor engine was the 1275 GT of 1970-1981. This engine had 1.312in/33.3mm diameter inlet valves and 1.156in/29.3mm exhaust valves. The exhaust valves being the same

as 1970-1971 Cooper S ones. The collets and valve spring retainers used on these engines were single groove components, as used on the Cooper S engines. The single valve springs used gave 70ib/32kg of seated pressure, and 105lb/48kg of over the nose pressure at 0.318in/8.1mm of valve lift. New valve springs had a free length of 1.960in/49.8mm. They would compress enough to allow 0.395in/10.0mm of valve lift.

METRO ENGINES

The A+ Metro and MG Metro 1300 engines are covered here because they are often fitted into Minis. These engines' cylinder heads also get fitted on to all manner of Mini engines. All that's necessary to make the engine change from a Metro to a Mini are Mini mounting brackets.

1300 Metro engine

The A+ Metro 1275cc engine went from 1980-1991. It used 1.312in/33.3mm diameter inlet valves and 1.156in/29.3mm diameter exhaust valves with triple groove valve stems and collets. The valve spring retainers were the raised ridge type shared with the 998cc A+ engines. The single valve springs used were as per the 1275 GT.

1300 MG Metro engine

The 1300 MG Metro used 1.400in/35.6mm head diameter inlet valves, and 1.156in/29.3mm head diameter exhaust valves, with triple groove stems/triple groove collets. The strong single valve springs gave a fitted height pressure of 75lb/34kg, and an over the nose pressure of approximately 110lb/48kg at 0.318in/8.0mm of valve lift. These valve springs allow approximately 0.395in/10.0mm of valve lift (maximum safe valve lift) and at this height give approximately 130lb/59kg of over the nose pressure.

When new, these valve springs allow 6500rpm.

The free length of these single valve springs when new is 2.050in/52.0mm. The black sintered valve spring retainers had the raised ridge on the top surface around where the two collets fit (the same ones as used on the standard 998cc and 1275cc A+ engines).

1300 MG Metro Turbo engine

The 1300 MG Metro Turbo engine is different from the other two A+ engines and all previous 1275cc engines. The exhaust valves on these engines were sodium filled, and they had a valve stem diameter of 0.313in/7.96mm. The inlet valves remained as per all others, with 0.279in/7.09mm diameter stems. The inlet valves had 1.312in/33.3mm head diameters, and the exhausts were the usual 1.156in/29.3mm.

The dual valve springs used on these engines are virtually the same as the original 1275 Cooper S springs of 1963-1971 (75lb/34kg of seated pressure and 140lb/64kg of 'over the nose' valve spring pressure at 0.318in/8.1mm of valve lift). Both valves used triple groove collets but these are different to suit the different valve stems. When refitting valves to engines, care is needed to make sure that the collets are paired correctly. That's two different sized valve stems, two different sized collets, and two types of valve spring retainer on the same cylinder head.

The exhaust valve spring retainers and triple groove collets used on this engine are unique to it, whereas the inlet ones are of the sintered type with the raised edge around the collet bore. The inlet valve triple groove collets are the same as those used on 998cc, 1275cc and Metro A+ engines.

The exhaust retainers are turned

MG Metro Turbo inlet valve spring retainer (sintered raised inner edge type) with triple groove collets on the left; and exhaust valve spring retainer with triple groove collets on the right.

from steel bar, while the inlet ones are black, raised-ridge sintered ones. The exhaust valve retainers have a square edge and a round groove machined in the top surface. This square edge makes for easy identification against the other two grooved top surface valve spring retainers as used on small bore engines.

The outer valve spring wire diameter of all large bore engines is 0.145in/3.70mm which is another way of positively identifying an outer valve spring for an A-series engine.

The inner valve spring wire diameter of the dual valve springs was 0.100in/2.5mm.

The entire range of standard fitted valve springs for A-series engines. Early 850cc (extreme left); later 850cc, and all 998cc and 1098cc single valve spring used (second left); twin carburettor 998cc and 1098cc engine dual valve springs (centre left); standard 1275cc single valve spring (centre right); Cooper S and MG Metro Turbo dual valve spring (second right); and 1300 MG Metro single valve spring (extreme right).

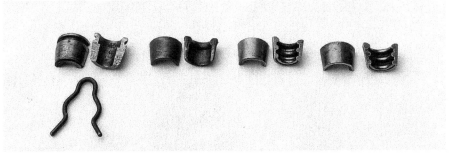

Early 850cc, 998cc and 1098cc collets and retaining circlip (left); later 850cc, 998cc, 1098cc and 1275cc single groove collets (centre left); A+ triple groove collets to suit 998cc and 1275cc engines (centre right); and MG Metro Turbo (A+) exhaust valve triple groove collets (right).

New Mini Cooper engines

Later 1275cc engines were those that came out in 1990 in the new Mini Cooper (A+ 1300 MG Metro specification engine). In 1993, they were fitted with single point fuel injection and, in 1998, they were fitted with twin point fuel injection with the last ones made in 2001. The bosses and fixings pertaining to carburettor type engines were deleted on these fuel injected engine blocks.

SUMMARY

This makes for a total of six valve spring combinations, 10 inlet valves, 7 exhaust valves, 7 different valve type spring retainers and 4 different collets over the entire range of A-series engines.

Small bore 848cc, 997cc, 998cc and 1098cc engines

3 types of inlet and exhaust valve
3 inlet valve head diameter (6 inlet valves)
1 exhaust valve head diameter (3 exhaust valves)
3 valve spring combinations
3 types of valve spring retainer
3 types of collet (two shared with the large bore engines)

Larger bore 970cc, 1071cc and 1275cc engines

2 types of inlet and exhaust valve
2 inlet valve head diameters (4 inlet valves)
2 exhaust valve head diameters (4 exhaust valves)
3 valve spring combinations
5 types of valve spring retainer
3 types of collet (two shared with the small bore engines)

The differences between the eight A-Series engine valve spring retainers makes it quite easy to positively identify all types at a glance (once you know what to look for).

Measuring the free length of new valve springs is a good idea but, of course, once valve springs have been used they start to reduce in free length. The longer they are used, the shorter they can become. To re-use valve springs they really do need to be the specified free length. If they are not they should be replaced. Checking the pressure at the installed height is ideal, but not everybody has access to this sort of equipment. If the valve springs you have are not to the required free length, replace them.

The entire range of collets and valve spring retainers. Top row: early 850cc, 998cc and 1098cc circlips, collets and valve spring retainer (grooved top chamfered outer edge). Second row: single groove collets, 1275cc valve spring retainer (left), Weslake 1275cc valve spring retainer (centre), later 850cc, 998cc and 1098cc single carburettor engine valve spring retainer (right). Third row: triple groove collets, an A+ 998cc and 1275cc 'raised inner edge' sintered valve spring retainer with a chamfered outer edge (left), an A+ 998cc and 1275cc A+ 'raised inner edge' sintered valve spring retainer with a radiused outer edge (centre), and a turned from steel round bar version of the same type (right). All three of these valve spring retainers are identical in size and are interchangeable. Fourth row: MG Metro Turbo A+ triple groove valve collets and valve spring retainer.

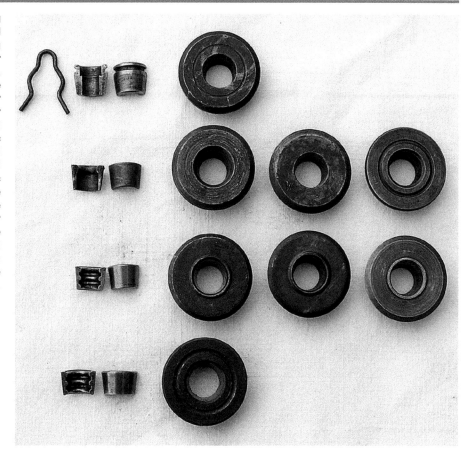

Chapter 4

Camshaft, timing chain & oil pump

CAMSHAFT CHOICE

Fitting a new or reground camshaft to replace a camshaft that's done 50,000 miles/80,000 kilometres, or more, is a sound idea. The reason for this is that the camshaft lobes wear and, as a consequence, lift reduces and so does the power of the engine. Of course, some camshafts will be quite worn at this distance, especially if the engine has not received many oil changes.

To check for worn camshaft lobes without stripping the engine, check the lift of each valve using the tail of a vernier caliper to see what the total amount of valve spring retainer movement is. This involves removing the rocker cover, setting the tappet clearance to the correct amounts and turning the engine so that each valve goes through a full opening and closing cycle. The quick way to do this is remove the sparkplugs and with the car on level ground and in top gear move the car along until each valve in turn is at full lift, put the handbrake

on and measure the valve movement. Expect the actual lift on average to be about 0.010in/0.25mm less than the workshop manual specified valve lift for camshaft lobes that are still 'on size' (within tolerance and not excessively worn).

For road use in almost all applications the ideal camshaft to use is the standard one already in your engine or a new replacement if yours is worn. The standard camshaft is fine in most instances because the engine revs that will be used will not exceed 6000rpm. While some standard camshafts are better than others, there are no bad standard cams. In almost all circumstances using the camshaft that your engine is equipped with as standard will result in an engine with good performance. The only things that detract significantly from power output when using the standard camshaft are camshaft lobe wear and/ or grossly retarded camshaft timing caused by timing chain wear.

The majority of standard camshafts fitted to A-Series engines have very similar lobe profiles with some slight variations of phasing: to all intents and purposes, all these cams can be regarded as being very similar in action. The better standard A-Series camshafts (in this instance meaning longer duration and slightly higher lift) such as the 1300 MG Metro camshaft are suitable for all applications for use up to 6000-7000rpm, depending on engine capacity. This is a very underrated camshaft.

For road use, camshafts with more duration than what the standard 1300 MG Metro unit or aftermarket equivalent replacement has are to be avoided as they offer no real improvement in all round usable acceleration and can be the cause of poor fuel consumption.

The most common standard camshaft found in pre-A+ 998cc and all 1098cc engines has 5-45-51-21 valve timing. This means that the inlet

Both of these camshaft lobes are standard Austin/Rover ones. The camshaft lobe on the left is from a standard 1275cc (narrow point lobe) while the camshaft lobe on the right is a 1300 MG Metro one (wider, fatter lobe). The 'action' of the 1300 MG Metro camshaft gives better cylinder filling (volumetric efficiency) and more power, but slightly higher fuel consumption.

valve opens 5 degrees before top dead centre (BTDC), and closes 45 degrees after bottom dead centre (ABDC), the exhaust valve opens 51 degrees before bottom dead centre (BBDC) and closes 21 degrees after top dead centre (ATDC). This camshaft is quite suitable for most road going applications 998cc and 1098cc A-Series engines. The inlet and exhaust valve lift is stated as being 0.285in/7.24mm with 0.275in/7.0mm being a more realistic figure.

Standard A+ 998cc engines have 9-41-49-11 valve timing and 0.318in/8.0mm inlet valve lift and 0.300in/7.6mm exhaust valve lift.

Standard A+ 1275cc engines have 9-41-55-17 valve timing, and the inlet and exhaust valve lift is 0.318in/8.0mm. Fitting an A+ 1275cc standard camshaft into an A+ 998cc engine is a good move (this camshaft is also used in 1300 MG Metro turbo engines).

The 1300 MG Metro and 1275 Sport engines have camshafts with 16-56-59-29 valve timing with both valves having 0.318in/8.0mm of lift, and no road going engine really needs more radical timing than this. This camshaft is an excellent 'drop in fit' for any 998cc or 1275cc A+ engine and can

be fitted into non A+ 850cc, 998cc or 1098cc engine with a bit of extra work. The inlet lobe profile of this camshaft is quite different to those found on standard 988cc/1275cc A+ and early narrow camshaft lobe 850cc/998cc/1098cc camshafts, and this is the factor that sets this camshaft apart from all other standard camshafts. Note that any pin- or star-drive camshaft/oil pump type A-Series engine can be converted to use a slot-drive camshaft and oil pump, but the conversion does require a kit and drilling of the block as well as having the engine out of the car and separated from the gearbox. Bear in mind that camshafts with the 1300 MG Metro profile are available from the likes of Piper Cams under the original camshaft specification codes '450' (pin-drive) and '500' (star-drive). This means that any A-Series engine can be fitted with 1300 MG Metro camshaft timing by substitution. The reason for doing the complete swap to a 'slot drive' oil pump is to gain the reliability afforded by the later system (it's the best standard drive system available).

Provided the camshaft you have fitted is in good condition, the

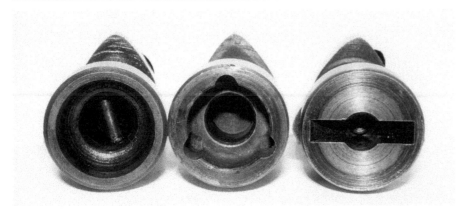

The three types of oil pump drive. From the left - pin, star and slot.

recommendation is to stay with it unless you are specifically looking for as much power from your engine as possible within the framework of being reasonably standard. This is because when your engine is tuned in the other areas detailed in this book (like all important ignition timing and cylinder head choice), it'll perform much better than you would imagine and will not have excessive fuel consumption.

Each of the standard camshafts is suitable for use in the particular engine capacity that it was designed for, but it's also quite acceptable to fit an A+ 1275cc camshaft to a 998cc A+ engine, while the 1300 MG Metro slot-drive camshaft is a 'drop-in fit' in any A+ A-Series engine (998cc or 1275cc).

The 1300 MG Metro camshaft is not a 'drop-in fit' in pre-A+ engines as the oil pump is slot-driven on A+ engines, whereas it had pin-drive or star-drive on earlier units. All pre A+ engines can be modified to take a slot-drive oil pump and camshaft. Aftermarket parts suppliers offer a spacer plate that packs the slot-drive oil pump out from the block, though extra holes must be drilled and tapped in the back of the block to accommodate this modification. Any engine reconditioner can do this work for you, but the engine does have to be removed from the car and the clutch, etc., removed from the engine.

There have been two lobe widths used on A-Series engines. The 850cc, 998cc and 1098cc engines had narrow lobes and wide lobes on their camshafts while, retaining the original timing figures, with the later engines' camshaft being wide lobe. When the 998cc engine was made A+ in 1980, the camshaft timing was changed to 9-41-49-11, and 0.300in/7.6mm of valve lift was specified (as opposed to 5-45-40-10 timing and 0.285in/7.24mm of valve lift). All 850cc and 1098cc engines had pin-drive oil pumps and so did 998cc engines until the A+ makeover and the advent of slot-drive in 1980. Early 1275cc engines had narrow camshaft lobes and pin-drive oil pumps until the late 1960s when the camshafts were made wide lobe and star-drive, which was retained until the A+ unit of 1980 was introduced. The reason Austin/Rover went to a wider lobed camshaft design was to improve the wear characteristics of the cam lobes. For road use, a narrow lobe standard camshaft can still be used with confidence, provided the valve spring pressure is not going to be any higher than standard. The camshaft should be new or correctly reground and the lifters new or reground. There is no doubt, however, that the wide lobe camshafts are better for durability.

There are three types of camshaft to oil pump drive: in order of

Slot-type oil pump driveshafts have been known to break at the point arrowed.

manufacture over the years they are pin-drive, star-drive and slot-drive.

All A+ engines have slot-drives and these are the best of the oil pump drive systems as they are the most reliable.

The star-drive is pretty reliable too, but more complicated. For higher performance applications, replacing the actual 'star' of the star-drive is required because it wears and breakage is possible after high mileages.

The pin-drive system is simple and was used with narrow lobe camshafts. Pin-drive systems are generally reliable but do have a tendency to break (drive tang of the oil pump) after high mileages. When this happens the engine is often ruined because of the instant loss of oil pressure. Anyone who has an engine with a pin-drive oil pump should consider replacing the oil pump as this is the best way of preventing drive failure through metal fatigue. Unfortunately, this does mean removing the engine from the car and partially dismantling it.

The best option by far is to convert to a slot-drive type camshaft and oil pump, but this does takes some engineering work. With a slot-drive

oil pump and camshaft fitted, you can forget about it as it will be extremely reliable.

Camshaft lift can be checked by measuring (with a vernier calliper) the distance each valve retainer moves from rest until the full lift point (maximum depression) is reached. Most camshaft lobes do not make the full manufacturer's claim so, provided the actual lift is not more than about 0.020in/5.08mm less than the specified amount, the camshaft is acceptable and serviceable.

Camshafts can be reground and it's quite possible to put an 1300 MG Metro camshaft profile on to a narrow lobe pin-drive camshaft. If the narrow lobe camshaft you have does not have excessively worn lobes or worn and scored bearing journals, then it will almost certainly 'take' a regrind and be as good as new afterwards. The camshaft grinder operator will automatically check all of this before grinding the camshaft.

There have been other original equipment camshaft profiles similar to the MG Metro 1300's over the years, such as the 997cc camshaft which had 16-56-51-21 valve timing. This was

With the dots on each sprocket lined up like this and the number one (front) piston at top dead centre, all engines will have correct basic timing.

a very good road going camshaft for any of the 850cc, 998cc or 1098cc A-Series engines, and is available as a regrind or new from Piper Cams or Kent Cams. From the original factory camshaft specifications ask for "948" in pin-drive, or "567" in star-drive form.

All of the original camshafts for A-Series engines are 'mild' as are the equivalent new camshafts offered by the aftermarket manufacturers. Anything 'wilder' than standard results in a lumpy idle and a degree of 'camminess' which is not really ideal for road use: fuel consumption increases too.

There are several aftermarket camshafts which because of their low lift can be considered road going engines. For example the Kent Cams MD256 is fine for an 850cc, 998cc or 1098cc engine fitted with a 1275cc cylinder head (**Caution!** - provided exhaust valve to block deck clearance is checked). The MD256 camshaft is compatible with standard valve springs

and there are other similar low lift aftermarket camshafts available too.

Camshaft timing

Because this book is about the simplest way to achieve more performance from your Mini engine there is no recommendation to check the actual camshaft timing, although it is always a desirable thing to do.

Do make sure the dots of the sprockets are lined up when fitting the timing chain otherwise camshaft timing will be wrong. If your engine does not perform as expected, the problem could be retarded camshaft timing: unfortunately, because the factory timing marks have been relied upon, there is no real way of knowing whether the problem (grossly advanced or retarded camshaft timing) is there or not. In most instances the standard timing marks will see the camshaft timing correct to within 2 or 3 degrees of the standard factory setting and for road use this is accurate

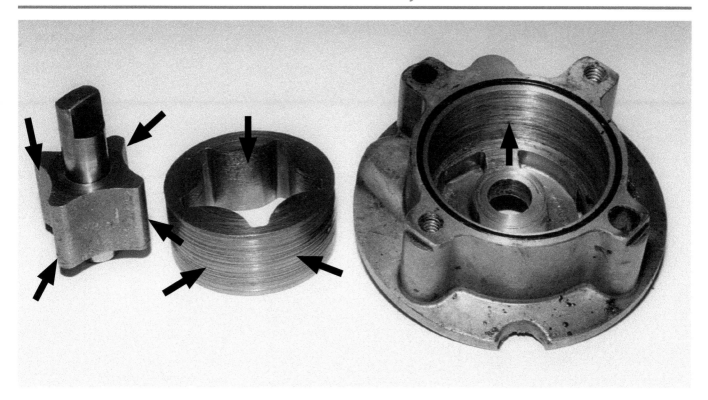

Internal parts of this oil pump are well worn with all surfaces scored. The rotors (left and centre) are worn undersized, while the pump body (right) is worn oversized.

enough, though not perfect. It is possible to have a major mismatch through the machining tolerances of various parts but most grossly inaccurate camshaft timing is caused by incorrect assembly (usually one tooth out).

If you want to know more about camshaft choice and precision timing there is another book in the SpeedPro Series also by Des Hammill called *How to Choose Camshafts & Time Them for Maximum Power*.

Summary
Retaining the standard camshaft for your particular engine is recommended. If your camshaft is checked and found to be in good condition (lift not reduced by wear) you can use it with confidence, knowing that it'll provide good engine performance up to 6000rpm. If, on the other hand, the camshaft is worn then there is no alternative but to replace

it: you could install a new/reground standard cam or an MG Metro 1300 one for extra performance (if you don't mind losing a few miles to the gallon and having some extra work done if your engine is not an A+ unit).

The 1300 MG Metro camshaft is a very underrated camshaft, and frequently gets replaced with something 'better'. In fact, the factory engineers developed this camshaft as the sensible limit for these road going engines. These camshafts are compatible with the valve gear, and are true 'drop in fit' items on 998 and 1275 A+ engines. This particular camshaft is one of the best all round, road going camshafts that have ever been available for the A-Series engine, either from the factory or from any aftermarket camshaft manufacturer's product range.

OIL PUMP
Caution! - Oil pumps can wear much

Double row or 'Duplex' chain on the left and single row or 'Simplex' chain on the right.

more than you might imagine. Just because the oil pump is pumping oil all of the time does not mean that it'll last forever. The problem for the oil pump is that it always has unfiltered oil going through it and this means that debris will pass through the pump before being removed by the filter. This is why when an oil pump is dismantled you'll often find it to be heavily scored on all surfaces. Frequently, particles embed themselves into the soft aluminium casing and then work away at the steel of the bi-rotor. All of the clearances of the pump enlarge over time and the pump gradually loses its efficiency. The result of this is lower oil pressure than standard, especially when the engine is warm. Whenever an engine is dismantled the oil pump should be renewed to preclude breakage of the drive and to maintain standard oil pressure.

The other aspect of maintaining oil pressure is of course the crankshaft bearing clearances. Once the bearing clearances have become larger than standard through wear, not even a new standard oil pump will be able to maintain the correct hot oil pressure. There comes a time when all engines need to be rebuilt and have new

bearings fitted to them to restore the correct clearances. In this regard the long stroke 1098cc engine is the main offender as its long stroke causes heavier main bearing and journal wear, especially the centre main bearing and journal.

TIMING CHAIN

The standard simplex (single row) chain is not really acceptable for higher performance applications. What happens is that the chain wears very quickly and while the engine still seems to run well, the camshaft timing retards as the chain wears.

While the simplex chain is adequate for a dead standard engine, an aftermarket duplex chain is better for engine efficiency. It is not uncommon for a standard engine which has covered 50,000 miles/80,000 kilometres to have an unbelievably loose and noisy timing chain. The noise is not really the problem of course, but the fact that the chain has worn so much means that the camshaft timing could be anything up to 10 degrees retarded. By comparison an aftermarket duplex timing chain and sprockets, which will hold the camshaft timing setting for

Typical duplex timing chain and sprocket set.

very much longer, represents excellent value for money.

The best option for higher performance applications is to fit a duplex (twin row) chain and sprockets. Duplex timing chains were once fitted as standard equipment by BMC and BLMC, but they no longer make replacement parts. Duplex timing chain and sprocket sets are readily available from aftermarket manufacturers and suppliers. If you already have a set of duplex sprockets, you can buy a new duplex chain from the same sources.

Unfortunately, fitting a duplex chain is not always straightforward. On some engines, A+ for example, there is a shroud inside the timing chain cover which has to be removed to provide clearance for the wider chain. For many people this is too much trouble and, in cases like these, the answer is to fit a genuine Austin/Rover replacement simplex chain, but be prepared to replace it at regular intervals (25,000 miles or 40,000 kilometres).

Caution! - Before fitting a duplex

timing chain, fit the duplex sprocket to the camshaft, tighten the nut and then see if the sprocket can be turned easily for at least one full revolution. The rocker shaft has to be removed to do this so that the camshaft sprocket can be turned by hand. The reason for making this check is to ensure that there is clearance between the back of the sprocket and the camshaft thrust plate and screws that protrude from the block.

Caution! - Replace the chain tensioner (if fitted) whenever the timing chain is changed.

Note that chain tensioners are not available from the makers of duplex timing chain sets. The factory used to make them in days gone by, but relatively low demand has meant that they've been phased out. It's okay to use the standard simplex (single chain) tensioner in conjunction with a duplex timing chain. The wear pattern is a bit odd after some use, but the simplex device does tension the duplex chain and is reliable.

PUSHRODS & ROCKER SHAFTS

Standard pushrods and standard rocker shafts are quite acceptable for any road use application. High ratio rockers on road going engines fitted with standard camshafts are not necessary and offer no improvement in usable power in this application.

LIFTERS (CAM FOLLOWERS)

Caution! - Always fit new or reground lifters with a new camshaft. A lifter which has pit marks in it is not fit to be reground. Lifters wear concavely on the surface that contacts the camshaft lobe. When new, lifters are actually slightly convex and not flat as you might imagine. Camshaft lobes are tapered so the lobes and the bases of new lifters match perfectly and will wear in harmony. One problem with all later 1275cc engines is, of course, that they didn't have tappet chest covers, and the only way to get to the lifters was by dismantling the entire engine. Early 1275 engines had tappet chest covers, like all small bore engines.

Chapter 5

Ignition system

One of the most significant factors contributing to an improvement in the performance of any A-Series engine is reworking the ignition system as described in this chapter to alter the system's mechanical advance characteristics. Failure to attend to this aspect of an engine is one of the biggest causes of a lack of engine performance and general disappointment with modified engines. The amount of power loss when the ignition system is wrong is totally disproportionate to the amount of work it actually takes to get the whole thing right.

There are two types of Lucas ignition system for the A-Series engine: the original contact breaker points type and, later, electronic ignition systems. Both standard ignition systems work well insofar as they are both reliable and produce a sufficient amount of spark to fire any mixture likely to be encountered in any road going application. Points type distributors

however do have the constant problem of contact breaker points wear.

There are two drive types for distributors and two distributor locking methods (A+ uses a clamp). Positively identify the model of distributor fitted to your engine before buying another distributor.

Before all else, the ignition system must be in perfect condition, with the quality of the spark at maximum. Nothing less will do. This means fitting new plug wires (HT leads) with no more than 10kV ohms of resistance, new sparkplugs, new distributor cap, new points, new condenser, and a new standard recommended/rated coil. The coil has to be of the right output specification if the points are to be absolutely reliable. In the case of an electronic ignition system, fit a new and tested, or used and tested, module and coil.

You can't fit any old coil to a points type distributor-equipped engine. Electronic ignition coils are

what are termed 'high energy' coils, and are unsuitable for points type ignitions as they'll destroy the contacts of the points. Be sure to get the right rated standard coil for a points type ignition. An electronic ignition system can be used successfully with most coils, but even so, it's advisable to fit the recommended output rated coil.

THE IMPORTANCE OF IGNITION ADVANCE

The power loss and lack of overall engine efficiency caused by not having sufficient ignition advance in one of these A-Series engines is almost unbelievable.

A standard distributor with suitable advance bobweight springs and set to give 34-35 degrees total mechanical advance will give good top end engine performance and could give ideal low speed (3000rpm and below) engine performance too: unfortunately, low speed engine performance could also be absolutely dreadful. The reason for this is that there is such a wide range of mechanical advance built into the distributors by Lucas.

Test your engine for acceleration with 34 and 35 degrees of total mechanical advance. Use the setting that gives the best acceleration. (Note: although, in many instances, 32 degrees will give as much power as 34 or 35 degrees of total advance, an engine set with 34-35 degrees of total advance will usually accelerate the car quicker). Always use the maximum amount of advance possible (**Caution!** - without 'pinking'), but no more than 35 degrees.

A 10 degree distributor incorporates 20 crankshaft degrees of advance. This means that a 10 degree mechanical advance distributor set at 15 degrees of static advance will have 35 degrees of static advance (15+20=35). The same distributor set at 14 degrees of static advance will have 34 degrees of static advance.

14 or 15 degrees may seem a large amount of static advance but, nevertheless, it is the requirement when good quality fuel is available. If the fuel available does not allow the engine to respond well to these settings, retard the ignition in 1 degree increments until it does respond. Use a 10 degree distributor in all instances.

Reference is made in this book to 'static' and 'idle' or 'idle speed' advance. There can be confusion here because the figures can be the same or different.

Static advance is the amount of advance that the engine has when it is not turning or is being turned over by the starter motor before it fires.

Idle speed advance is not quite the same because the rate at which the mechanism advances from its static setting depends on the strength of the two advance springs fitted to the particular distributor. It's quite

possible for a distributor to have an amount of idle speed advance the same as its static advance right up to about 1800rpm if the advance springs are quite strong (advance mechanism effectively not working). That same distributor fitted with quite weak springs could have 6-8 degrees of advance beyond the static setting at 1800rpm (advance mechanism working).

The distinction between 'mechanical advance' (or 'centrifugal advance') and 'vacuum advance' is fairly straightforward. Mechanical advance is created by bobweights in the distributor moving outward against spring tension under centrifugal force as engine revs increase. This movement rotates the distributor baseplate a little and in so doing progressively advances the timing. The vacuum system also rotates the distributor baseplate, but is governed by inlet manifold vacuum. Both systems are complementary to overall engine performance and economy, although only the mechanical advance is used during acceleration, which is why it has to be absolutely right. Vacuum advance affects the engine economy when not on full throttle (vacuum being generated by the engine) by increasing the total amount of advance in these conditions.

CONTACT BREAKER-TYPE DISTRIBUTORS

The main problem with most standard distributors is that the advance curve and the rate of advance are not suitable for optimised performance. There is only one solution and that's to fit an A-Series Lucas distributor which has 10 degrees of mechanical advance built in and to change the mechanical advance bobweight springs to give the required advance rate characteristics.

Note that there are two types of

distributor drive for A-Series engines, early and late. The late ones for A+ engines (1275cc and 998cc) only are 'wide slot;' all others are of 'narrow slot' type. Lucas made 10 degree distributors in all distributor versions, including the two electronic models: there has been a 10 degree distributor for every model of A-Series engine.

Scrapyards are the place to find 10 degree Lucas A-Series distributors and buy them cheaply. Identifying the timing characteristics will involve removing the breaker plate and looking at the numbers stamped on the advance mechanism: there is no other way. Most scrapyards are throwing these distributors away and seldom mind anyone taking the plate out to see what the amount of advance is. There has been quite a wide range of amounts of advance used in Lucas distributors over the years.

The advance springs fitted to the distributor control the rate of advance (in relation to engine revs) from static to total mechanical (centrifugal) advance. If you have a 10 degree distributor, all that has to be done is to change the strong advance spring for a weaker one.

Because this book deals with relatively simple 'bolt-on' performance tuning, serious distributor modification is outside its scope and distributor substitution is what is advocated. The Lucas distributor (as opposed to the Ducellier item) is recommended because it is the most common distributor fitted to A-Series engines and the easiest to find in scrapyards. It is quite possible to alter any Lucas (or Ducellier) points type or electronic distributor so that the mechanical advance is right for any engine. If you want more information there is another book in the SpeedPro series also written by Des Hammill and called *How to Build & Power Tune*

The advance mechanism spring at the top of the picture is the weaker of the two standard ones, while the spring at the bottom is a Ford Motorcraft one. The number nine stamped on this distributor refers to its nine degrees of advance. This, of course, converts to 18 degrees of advance at the crankshaft.

This distributor has 10 degrees of mechanical advance built into signified by the number 10 stamped on the advance plate. That's 20 crankshaft degrees of advance.

Distributor-type Ignition Systems.

For the amount of work involved in changing the distributor and one of its springs, and marking the crankshaft damper or pulley so that the engine can be accurately strobe light timed, the improvement in engine performance is totally disproportionate. No A-Series engine will give optimum road going performance with a

Two light Ford Motorcraft distributor mechanical advance springs. The spring on the left has had its eyes 'tweeked' using long-nosed pliers to reduce the overall length of the spring and so increase its effective tension when fitted into a Lucas distributor. It doesn't take too much reworking of the spring to achieve the right tension.

standard distributor set in the standard position (2, 3 ,4 or 5 degrees of static ignition timing).

The total advance in almost all instances will need to be 34 or 35 degrees. **Caution!** - when this amount of advance proves to be too much, the engine almost always has too much compression for the octane rating of the fuel being used.

Reducing the amount of ignition advance to stop an engine with too much CR for the available fuel 'pinking' ('pinging') is the wrong way to go. Compression is not the main criteria for any A-Series engine, but optimum burning of the air/fuel mixture certainly is. It's better to have slightly too little compression than slightly too much because when there is too much CR the engine cannot be accelerated hard with ideal ignition advance because of 'pinking.'

Advance springs

The two standard centrifugal advance springs found in all standard application Lucas distributors are collectively too firm. The lightest advance spring can remain in the distributor while the heavy (secondary) advance spring is the one that is removed and replaced with an alternative. There is one mechanical advance spring from another distributor which is for the 10 degree Lucas distributor and that's the light (primary) advance spring from a Motorcraft distributor as used on

Ford Crossflow engines and SOHC 'Pinto' engines. There are thousands of Motorcraft distributors in scrapyards and each one has the required light advance springs.

The particular Motorcraft distributors concerned were found on SOHC engines in Cortinas, Transits and Capris up to 1982, in all Crossflow-powered Escorts up to 1980 and Fiestas up to 1982. These springs are no longer officially available from Ford dealers, but suitable springs had the following part numbers: 1473378, 1799737, 1489557 and 1579229. It is just possible that some Ford dealers might still have a spring or two in stock (old stock).

The tensions of these Motorcraft primary springs varied slightly from engine model to engine model, with some springs being of slightly different wire diameter (0.025 or 0.030in/0.6 or 0.7mm) and overall length. The stronger of these 'light' Ford springs is the ideal spring for the A-Series application.

The spring eyes will need to be tweaked to make the thinner wire springs effectively a bit stronger and more suitable for this new application. The average length of a Motorcraft distributor's weaker advance spring is about 0.690in/17.5mm. The length can be altered using fine point, long-nosed pliers so that the spring ends up a minimum of $1/8$in/3.2mm shorter than it was originally. Sometimes the spring can be made a little bit shorter again (0.525in/14.3mm overall length) depending on how close to the coils the wire is gripped before bending the eyes. It often pays to have a couple of springs just in case a spring is ruined when altering it.

Advance spring tension is used to control the engine speed at which maximum mechanical (centrifugal) advance is achieved. Weaker springs allow the advance to be 'all in' at a lower rpm than stronger springs. There is no application that requires the total advance to be all in before 2500rpm nor later than 3500rpm. Having total mechanical ignition advance as early as possible within the 2500-3500rpm range is the ideal situation. **Caution!** - Having the engine 'pinking' during full throttle acceleration from off idle is not ideal (engine damage will eventually result) and indicates that stronger springs are needed. The usual rev range in which the advance will be all in is between 2700 and 3300rpm. Road testing is the only way to find out what the right setting (combined spring tension) is for your individual application.

Contact breaker points

The contact breaker points system does have the age old problem of points wear, but this won't prove to be all that detrimental on the road and, realistically, only means that the points do have to be replaced every so often. Unfortunately the quality of points sets does tend to leave a bit to be desired and some times the 'life' of a set of points can be very short. The average life (remaining in first class condition) of a set of points seems to be in the region of just 1000-5000 miles/1600-8000km.

Always carry a spare set of new points in your car, and a stubby screwdriver, and make sure you know how to change the points.

Always reset the ignition timing after fitting a new set of points, as there are slight differences between sets, and the advance could be 2-3 degrees different if you just substitute one set of points for another (resulting in power loss through being slightly retarded, or pinking through being over advanced).

Don't change the condenser as a matter of course every time the points are changed, rather change the condenser when the points contacts pit too quickly (1000 miles/1600km, or less.

Coil

Use a standard voltage rating coil in all instances. If the points contacts become pitted very quickly, have the voltage output of the coil tested and change the condenser.

Note that having a coil with the right output matters for the points type distributor system. Fitting a higher than standard rating coil sometimes leads to an engine misfire. Check to see what coil the distributor you are using was designed to run with, and don't use anything else.

Note that it's not necessary to change the condenser every time the points in a distributor are changed. If the contact anvils of the contact breaker points removed from the distributor are worn equally, the condenser is working well and should not be changed. However, if the points have a pointed section on one of the contact anvils (looks like a miniature mountain) and a hollow on the opposing contact anvil (looks like a miniature crater), the condenser is faulty in the sense that it is not operating with design specified capacity: change the condenser in such circumstances.

ELECTRONIC DISTRIBUTORS

There have been two types of

electronic distributor made by Lucas for A-Series engines. The early one (59 DM4) was pretty much a conversion of the early points type distributor to a breakerless distributor (1982 to 1984). The mechanical advance mechanism of this unit is in the normal place and works as per previous Lucas distributors. These distributors are not common but, if used in a higher performance application, need to be 10 degree mechanical advance versions. The very strong advance spring must be removed and replaced with a weaker spring (the same procedure as for an original contact breaker points type distributor).

The second, later, and much more common Lucas electronic distributor (65 DM4) is slightly different in design and construction with a one piece spindle (1985 and on). The mechanical advance mechanism is in the casing and moves the pick-up and is not like previous Lucas distributors made for A-Series engines.

Another factor with these later 65 DM4 distributors is that the advance mechanism springs are totally different from almost all other distributors in their design, and they're almost unbelievably strong. The strong spring will have to be replaced but the problem is finding replacement springs of suitable strength and length to allow full mechanical advance to be achieved between 2800rpm and 3300rpm.

It's possible to just remove the stronger spring (thicker coil wire) of the two from the mechanical advance mechanism and use only the weaker spring to control the mechanical advance (or two weak springs from similar distributors). It all depends on the strength of the particular spring and whether it allows full advance within the correct rev range (checked with a strobe light and a degree marked crankshaft damper/pulley). With the standard set-up, the two springs are only both in operation at over 3000rpm: the combination allows the distributor to continue to advance up to 5000rpm.

Having only one spring in the 65 DM4 electronic distributor is an acceptable solution, but if you can find two springs which provide the required advance characteristics, this is the preferred option.

The weaker spring used in some Jaguar XK engine Lucas distributors can be fitted to 65 DM4 distributors, but note that two are needed and the elongated eye will have to be tweaked to effectively lengthen the spring and reduce the tension so that ignition is

fully advanced between 2800rpm and 3300rpm.

No application will need the total mechanical advance to be 'all in' earlier than 2500rpm with 2700-2800rpm being the usual. Any earlier than 2500rpm and the engine will likely 'pink' ('ping') under load (reduction in power when this is happening). If an engine 'pinks' with the ignition fully mechanically advanced at 2500rpm use progressively stronger springs until the 'pinking' stops.

Advance characteristics (controlled by spring tension) can be checked using a strobe light provided the crankshaft damper has been suitably marked at 14, 15, 34 and 35 degrees

This accurately drawn and sized diagram can be copied and the copy fixed to the front face of the crankshaft damper/pulley using adhesive. (You'll find two more copies on page 99 which you can cut from the book).

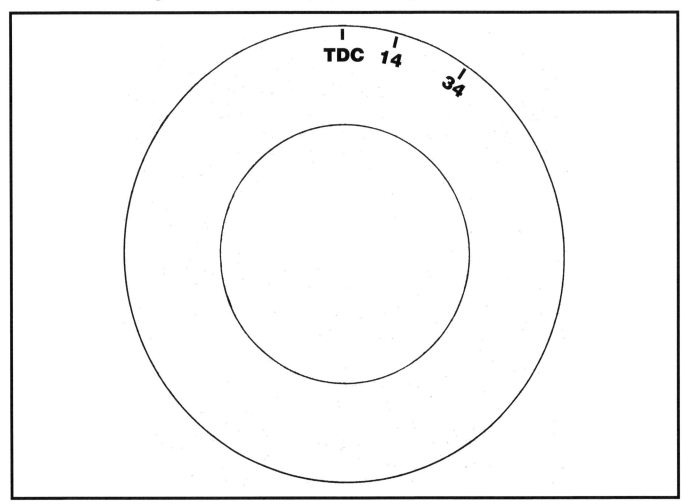

Engine at top dead centre (TDC). This damper has been permanently marked for 34 degrees, 14 degrees and TDC.

Engine at 14 degrees before top dead centre (TDC).

before top dead centre (BTDC). The ignition timing will advance from idle as engine rpm is increased until full advance is reached at a particular engine speed. Consider 2500rpm to be the absolute minimum and 3500rpm the maximum engine speed for full

mechanical (centrifugal) advance to occur (all distributors).

Both electronic distributors are excellent for use in higher performance engines with the advantage of the complete absence of 'points bounce,' irrespective of engine rpm.

Engine at 34 degrees before top dead centre (TDC).

The standard points are definitely acceptable for operation up to 6500rpm, but will break down at some stage above this engine speed.

The only thing likely to affect reliability of these electronic distributors is module failure. The solution to this potential problem is to always have on hand a new replacement module which (even though new) has been tested to make sure that it is working correctly. Note that many parts suppliers now test any module that they sell before they sell it to avoid comebacks from people who do not fit them correctly. Leaving things off like the 'jelly' (heat conduction silicone grease) that goes between the back of the module and the side of the distributor, for example, on later distributors, or the car body on earlier distributors. Modules do fail from time to time and it pays to keep a spare in the car. The engine will not go without one, and it only takes two minutes to change one.

VACUUM ADVANCE SYSTEM

A road going engine uses vacuum advance to get the best economy, therefore no road going engine should be without a vacuum advance mechanism. This means that when an engine is revving at more than 4000rpm, on a motorway, for example, with inlet manifold vacuum present, there could be anything from 35 - 45 degrees of total advance operating in the engine, depending on the loading (vacuum being produced). When you put your foot down to accelerate the vehicle, the vacuum drops to zero (and the vacuum advance drops to zero degrees) and the engine relies on the mechanical advance built into the distributor.

CHECKING IGNITION TIMING

Caution! - The rate of spark advance must be checked using a strobe light in conjunction with a degree marked crankshaft pulley or damper rim, and there must be a minimum of three marks. The first is the top dead centre (TDC) mark, the second is the idle advance mark (14 or 15 degrees) and the third is the total advance degrees mark (34 or 35 degrees). You can incorporate all five markings if you wish. With the pulley/damper rim marked and the engine idling (vacuum advance disconnected) the strobe light will show the idle advance and, as the engine speed is increased, the rpm point at which total mechanical advance is reached.

Never ever take it for granted that the original factory top dead centre (TDC) pulley/damper mark of any A- Series engine is accurate. Most will be accurate, but for various reasons a significant number won't be. If the TDC mark is not correct, and it is used as a reference point, the chances of the particular engine ever being tuned correctly are very slim indeed. The importance of optimum ignition timing on any A-Series engine cannot be over stressed.

The crankshaft damper or pulley must be carefully checked to see that the TDC mark is accurate and, if necessary, be re-marked if it is found to be out of position. Then the static and total advance timing marks are accurately added using the TDC mark as a datum. The correct way to test the accuracy of the TDC mark is to remove the sparkplug of the number one cylinder and use a long stem dial test indicator (dial gauge) to measure the point of maximum upward piston travel and relate that to the marks on the crankshaft damper or pulley. Many garages have the necessary equipment to do this and all engine reconditioners/ machine shops will have it.

A quick and easy way of putting timing marks on to an engine is to cut out a piece of cardboard to the exact shape and size of the accompanying diagram for the distributor you have and the timing you're going to use. While the cardboard will not last forever it will last for a reasonable amount of time. The TDC point is the datum point for fixing (gluing) the cardboard onto the damper or pulley. This is a quick easy and accurate method of marking the damper or pulley.

In terms of performance, ignition timing is one of the most significant alterations made to an engine. An engine can have the best camshaft, the best carburetion money can buy and the best of everything else that money can buy but, if the ignition is not timed correctly and the spark is insufficient in terms of quality (kilovolts), the engine simply will not perform at its full potential.

A strobe light must be used to check and set the ignition timing as this method shows the actual dynamic ignition timing (all variables are removed). Important! - The vacuum advance mechanism must always be disconnected when an engine is strobe light timed. If it isn't, the engine might well show more advance than is provided by the mechanical advance system alone. When an engine is accelerating hard under load there is no manifold vacuum and, as a consequence, the vacuum advance system is not working. The centrifugal advance built into the distributor is what the engine accelerates with and if the amount of advance is wrong, the engine will not accelerate as well as it should.

Set the total ignition advance to 34-35 degrees before top dead centre (BTDC) - whichever allows the car to accelerate quickest. Don't exceed 35 degrees of total mechanical advance as engine efficiency, and therefore power, reduces after this point.

Chapter 6

Fuel & octane ratings

The vast majority of fuels commercially available around the developed world these days are unleaded, and the octane rating of these fuels ranges from 90 to 98.3 RON (as of 2005). The last of the tetraethyl-leaded fuels were, on average, 93-98 RON octane, but they have now gone from all developed countries of the world, even for motor racing purposes. There are two basic tests used worldwide to determine the octane ratings of petrol/gasoline used in cars. These two test methods are the Research Octane Number (RON) and the Motor Octane Number (MON).

In the late 1920s, the Co-operative Fuels Research Council (CFR) in the USA devised a fuel sample testing method for determining the octane ratings of petrol/gasoline mixes. A very special single cylinder engine was made which had variable compression ratio and ignition timing (commonly referred to as a CFR engine). This very same engine is still used to test fuel samples for RON and MON using two different testing regimes or methods. Before a fuel sample is tested, the CFR engine is calibrated using a pure chemical mix 'reference fuel', which, because of its specific chemical content, is guaranteed to be 100 octane.

A sample of fuel to be tested is then used to run the engine. The RON method of obtaining an octane rating sees the CFR engine run at 600rpm with a set amount of ignition timing, as prescribed by ASTM D2699/IP237 (13 degrees Before Top Dead Centre). This rating is regarded as being representative of how the particular fuel will cause an engine to go at start up and idle. ASTM stands for American Society for Testing and Materials, and D2699 is the criteria of its RON test. IP stands for Institute of Petroleum, and 237 is its number for this testing regime (same test).

The same sample of fuel is again used to run the engine and the MON method of obtaining an octane rating is conducted under ASTM D2700/IP236 criteria. The CFR engine is run at 900rpm, the compression ratio is increased, and the ignition timing is advanced. The octane derived from this test is regarded as being representative of how the particular fuel sample will cause an engine to go on the road at cruise conditions or motorway driving. You virtually never see a MON rating displayed on a pump in a service station, but the two ratings are used by all petrol companies around the world. BS4040, for example, lists a minimum requirement for both RON and MON, but you only ever see the RON rating displayed on a pump.

At the time of writing (2005), the UK still has some leaded fuel available to motorists/enthusiasts. When tetraethyl-lead fuel was phased out in 2000, the British Government allowed 1% of the total amount of petrol made and sold in the UK to be leaded. The petrol companies which decided to

Exhaust valve seat in a head used with unleaded fuel for many miles: massive deterioration is obvious. All the exhaust valve seats in this head were the same. This is not valve seat recession, it is valve seat deterioration. Valve seat recession is the next stage, as the original valve seat has not been completely eroded away yet.

make this fuel and appoint selected outlets to sell it, used 0.099 grams per litre of tetraethyl-lead which provides acceptable valve seat protection and the fuel is 98 RON/86.2 MON.

Two unleaded fuels have been available in the UK for some time now, and these are Premium unleaded, which is required under BS7070 (British Standard 7070) to have a minimum RON of 95, and Super unleaded, which is required to have a minimum RON of 97. There is a slight problem with Super unleaded, however, if the petrol station holding it in its tanks is not a busy one. Super unleaded gets its extra octane by having various 'volatiles' mixed into it, and they tend to evaporate quite quickly. The longer the fuel remains in the tanks of the petrol station, the less the octane rating of the fuel. Premium unleaded does not have these 'volatiles' in it and, as a consequence, maintains its manufactured octane (95) rating longer. Because of this, Premium unleaded will, in some instances, cause your car to go better than

Super unleaded. As with all petrol/gasoline, if maintaining the octane is important (if you're using a high compression engine, for example), the fresher the fuel the better, and the recommendation is to buy your fuel from a busy forecourt. Old Super unleaded fuel can end up with a lower octane than Premium 95 in certain circumstances. The highest octane unleaded fuel commercially available in the UK today (2005) is Shell Optimax, which is 98.3 RON and 86.9 MON.

The USA, while still using the RON and MON tests to rate fuel, has taken this all one step further by introducing an Anti-Knock Index (AKI) number, based on the RON and the MON added together and then divided by 2. Other names for this system you see used in the USA are PP (Pump Posted) or perhaps PON (Pump Octane Number). As you can see, when you're talking octane, you need to be quite clear what criteria are being used.

In the USA there are three basic grades of AKI street legal unleaded

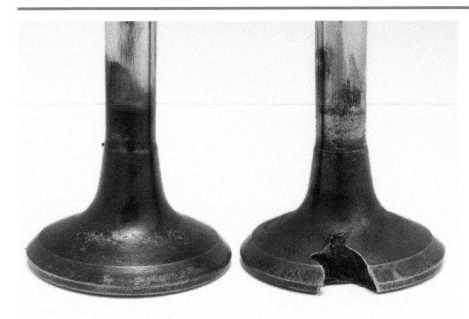

The valve on the right came out of the combustion chamber shown in the opposite photo and the valve on the left from the adjacent combustion chamber.

fuels on sale at the pumps, with slight variations in the Premium unleaded fuels, plus a very low octane Regular unleaded (New Mexico 85 AKI octane). For the purposes of matching the fuel available to a compression ratio that will be suitable, use the RON ratings of the US fuels listed. Take it that, on average, Regular unleaded 87 octane is suitable for use with 8.3-8.8:1 compression engines, Mid-grade unleaded 89 octane is suitable for use with 8.8-9.2:1 compression engines, and Premium unleaded 91 AKI octane is suitable for use with 9.0-9.3:1 compression engines. Add 0.3 for 92 AKI octane and 0.7 for 93 AKI octane.

Regular unleaded   87 octane is 91 RON - 83 MON
Mid-grade unleaded 89 octane is 94 RON - 84 MON
Premium unleaded   91 octane is 96 RON - 86 MON
or   92 octane is 97 RON - 87 MON
or   93 octane is 98 RON - 88 MON

For high octane street legal unleaded fuels, and for 'off road' racing purposes, USA enthusiasts are fortunate compared to those in other countries around the world, because there is a vast array of specially mixed and blended fuels available (for details of VP products go to www.vpracingfuels.com; the products of Sunoco can be viewed at www.sunoco.com; for F&L Racing Fuel products go to www.fandl.com; and for Sports Racing Gasoline products see www.cosbyoil.com).

If you look at the USA's Sunoco GT100 street legal unleaded fuel, for example, which is advertised as being 100 octane, is 105 RON and a 95 MON, making it a pretty good fuel for road use. The 100 octane rating you see advertised is the AKI, which is 105 + 95 divided by 2 = 100. This fuel will run a naturally aspirated A-Series engine with a compression ratio of 12.5:1 without any problem. Sunoco also makes an unleaded fuel called GT Plus, which has RON and MON values of 109 and 99, respectively, giving a 104 AKI, and will run a racing

engine with a compression ratio of 14:1 without problems. VP C10 Performance Unleaded is an equivalent fuel to Sunoco GT100, and the street legal VP Motorsport 103 is equivalent to Sunoco GT Plus. USA owners of 'soft' A-Series cylinder heads would need to use a lead substitute additive with these fuels to prevent valve seat recession.

Sunoco makes 'Standard Leaded' for racing purposes, and this has RON and MON ratings of 115 and 105 MON, respectively, and 0.99 grams of tetraethyl-lead per litre. Next is 'Supreme Leaded', which has RON and MON values of 114 and 110 MON, respectively, and 1.12 grams of tetraethyl-lead per litre. Finally there is 'Maximal Leaded' which has RON and MON ratings of 118 and 115, respectively, and 1.32 grams of tetraethyl-lead per litre. VP and Sports Racing Gasoline make equivalents. These sorts of leaded fuels will run any A-Series racing engine extremely well. All of these specialist racing fuels are excellent, but they are quite expensive.

For the benefit of older cars not designed to run on unleaded fuel, Britain introduced lead replacement petrol (LRP) in 2000, when tetraethyl-leaded fuels were phased out. LRP was 95 RON octane unleaded fuel with potassium added at the rate of 8 parts per million. It was claimed that LRP offered near equal valve seat recession protection to that of tetraethyl-lead fuel. Certainly, for all round general use, engines did not suffer from valve seat recession while using it. LRP was not overly suitable for high load situations, however, such as when an engine is driven at wide open throttle for long distances, though the petrol companies did state this at the time of the fuel's introduction. LRP fuel is not as common today as it used to be, and likely to be phased out completely within a few years.

HEADS WITHOUT HARDENED EXHAUST VALVE SEATS

Some countries still offer leaded fuel. The UK, for instance, still allows the production and sale of leaded fuel to garages that are prepared to stock it and sell it, on the basis that the amount of fuel sold nationwide is not more than 0.5% of the total amount of fuel sold. This means that leaded fuel is reasonably readily available for those people prepared to pay a premium price for it.

At 0.149 grams per litre, the amount of tetraethyl-lead in this fuel is quite small, but it did comply with BS4040. In the days of 5 Star fuel (mid-1950s, 1960s and 1970s) there was up to 3 grams of tetraethyl-lead per gallon. By the time 4 Star fuel was phased out, however, in 2000, BS4040 called for the amount of tetraethyl-lead content per litre to range from 0.05 to 0.150 grams. The major fuel companies opted for 0.149 grams per litre, keeping the tetraethyl-lead content right on the limit, in an effort to produce the best fuel possible within the confines of the standard. Many people may recall that some UK supermarkets were selling cheap fuel in the 1990s, with 0.05 grams of tetraethyl-lead per litre and approximate 92-93 RON octane rating. Anyone who used this fuel may have noticed getting a bit more fuel for their money, but probably a 20-25% drop in fuel economy. This was the very minimum of tetraethyl-lead allowed within the BS4040 standard, but was just enough by all accounts to stop valve seat recession.

Over a period of 5 years, I have

This 998cc engine's valve seat is badly recessed. The seat is now about ¹⁄₁₆in/1.5mm lower than it was as originally machined, and if reused with unleaded fuel it would get worse. The only thing to do now is to fit hardened valve seat inserts which will restore the cylinder head to better than new condition.

conducted a series of experiments using unleaded fuel in two A-Series engines which didn't have hardened valve seats fitted. In each case, the valve seats had done a lot of service, but the valves were still in good condition. Although the valve seats were regularly inspected, they were not reground or refurbished in any way. With both cylinder heads already having covered about 75,000 miles/ 120,000km on leaded fuel, they were put back into service. Both engines ran 10,000 and 25,000 miles/16,000 and 40,000km, respectively, and neither cylinder head failed in the more-or-less identical light duty applications (2500-3500rpm non-motorway applications). The 1275cc cylinder head, however, did show major signs of deterioration after being subjected to 10,000 miles/16,000km. The 998cc engine was subjected to the very same sort of treatment (same driver doing the same thing day after day) and did 25,000 miles/40,000km. The valve seats in this

engine's cylinder head were virtually the same as they were at the start of the test and could have gone on. There was some deterioration, but it was minimal, and followed the usual pattern for these engines.

Both engines had efficient cooling systems and were operating at similar water temperatures (78-80 degrees C/172-175 degrees F). This is an important point, as high engine operating temperatures make a difference, as the higher the temperature the worse the deterioration). The 998cc cylinder head, with more material around the exhaust valve and an engine which generates less heat, fared much better than the 1275 head.

Caution! - It's not possible to run an A-Series engine without hardened valve seat inserts on unleaded fuel at full throttle for miles and miles on a motorway under near maximum loading and get away with it. There will be some damage, but it takes considerable time to severely damage the cylinder head and ruin the valves and valve seats. The later the cylinder head the worse the damage and the faster it occurs (because the later heads are made of softer cast iron).

Caution! - An A-Series engine which doesn't have hardened exhaust valve seats fitted to it must be run on either lead-replacement fuel (LRP), tetraethyl-leaded 4 Star fuel if it's available, or unleaded fuel with an additive mixed with it. There is some variation in the effectiveness of the approved additives which are available, but none are as good as having the known recommended amount of tetraethyl-lead in the fuel. The approved additives offer a measure of protection and, for general road going driving, they all seem to offer sufficient protection. Some have octane boosting properties as well.

Caution! - The use of unleaded fuel in A-Series engines without hardened valve seats will result in deterioration of the seats and valves at a rate commensurate with the way the car is driven. Even a car driven around town all of the time at slow speeds and low engine loading will show some deterioration over, say, 10,000miles/16,000km, but the damage will not necessarily be major and the valve sealing not necessarily impaired. However, take the same car and travel at full speed for hour upon hour and the valves will quickly start to recess. Expect major damage after 2000miles/3200km of this sort of treatment (possibly a written-off cylinder head, with severe damage to the two inner exhaust valve seats). Expect the deterioration to start immediately with this sort of treatment but not necessarily show up until 2000miles/3200km have been covered (perhaps a bit more). Expect an engine which already has poor exhaust valve

seating to fail much quicker. It's the heat that does the damage ...

The range of fuel additives includes Superblend Zero Lead 2000, Redex 4 Star, Wynns, Millers VSP Plus, Valve Master and Red Line. There are plenty of others but none of them seem to be capable of being used in a real heavy duty application like motor racing. The only exception is TetraBOOST, which is not in quite the same category as the other additives. Anyone using an existing modified A-Series cylinder head, which has big valves, and which can't have hardened exhaust valve seats fitted to it, needs to add TetraBOOST to the unleaded fuel for maximum valve seat protection and its RON octane boosting properties. TetraBOOST has 1.23% tetraethyl-lead in it per litre, as well as 0.356% dibromoethane, and 0.385% dichoroethane, all in a solution of naphtha light aromatic. It's FBHVC (Federation of British Historic Car Clubs) tested and approved (2001). Mixed with 95 RON octane unleaded at the minimum recommended proportions, the combination becomes equivalent to 97 RON octane leaded fuel as per BS4040. Mixed with Shell Optimax 98.3 RON octane unleaded fuel at the minimum recommended proportions, the combination is equivalent to 100 RON octane leaded 4 Star fuel. Increase the amount of additive to 98.3 RON octane Shell Optimax, and the RON octane number increases to over 100, with up to 105-106 RON octane fuel being possible, but a lot of additive will be required to achieve this. You can get more information on TetraBOOST from Nik Cookson, TetraBOOST Ltd., 17 West Hill, London, SW19 1RB (Tel: +44 (0) 208 870 9933, Web: www.tetraboost. com.

The overall impact of the loss of leaded fuel is that regrinding valves

and valve seats may end up becoming a more frequent practice, as might the replacement of exhaust valves. Engines with perfect valve seating produce optimum engine power and engines with anything less don't. Using a cylinder head which has pit marks in the exhaust valve seats is just no good at all as it leads to premature valve seat failure. Nothing can be 'got away with' when it comes to exhaust valve seating on A-Series engines: once a valve seat is damaged it usually takes quite a lot of regrinding to restore it. This can only be taken so far before either valve seat inserts have to be fitted, a slightly larger diameter exhaust valve has to be fitted, or the cylinder head is scrapped.

Fitting hardened valve seats
Fitting hardened valve seats is an option once the original seats are damaged and is, of course, the solution to being able to use unleaded fuel without additives. Unleaded cylinder heads are available as outright purchases from Mini specialists or your own engine's cylinder head can have hardened valve seats fitted to it by your local engine reconditioner/machine-shop. Once a cylinder head has been fitted with hardened valve seats, unleaded fuel can be used without risk of valve seat recession. The fitting of hardened exhaust valve seats is a one off cost and being able to use straight unleaded fuel out of the pump makes for uncomplicated motoring. One thing that should always be done when converting your own cylinder head is to fit brand new exhaust valves.

While fitting hardened exhaust valve seats removes one problem, you do need to be aware of the fact that unleaded fuel is extremely hard on exhaust valves and no exhaust valve is going to last as long in an unleaded fuel engine as in a leaded fuel engine of years gone by. Expect exhaust valve contact area (seat) deterioration at a much greater rate than normal with 45,000 - 60,000miles/75,000 - 95,000km being the useful life of an exhaust valve. While it's possible to regrind the original valves, events will prove that it's more prudent to replace them.

CYLINDER HEADS WITH HARDENED EXHAUST VALVE SEATS

All Metros and Minis from 1989 on (998cc and 1275cc engines only) were fitted with hardened exhaust valve seats by the factory, and these cylinder heads can use unleaded fuel with impunity. In the UK, many of these cars are now being scrapped, and getting the cylinder heads off these cars engines is the cheapest way of getting an unleaded cylinder head. Most scrapyard owners will keep an eye out for the applicable registration number vehicles and let you know when a suitable car comes in if you ask them to. In a few years, these engines will be gone, and enthusiasts will have to convert. The time to collect Mini parts like this is now.

Caution! - If an engine fitted with hardened exhaust valve seats is excessively overheated (radiator failure for example) or a valve seat not installed in the cylinder head correctly, the seats can come loose which will cause engine damage. While this is an unlikely eventuality, it is certainly possible ...

Chapter 7

Compression ratio (CR)

Using the highest compression ratio (CR) compatible with the octane rating of the fuel being used is a well founded principle. The general range of fuel octanes available worldwide is from 90 to 98, on average, with the later unleaded fuels, such as the 98.3 RON octane Shell Optimax, for example, costing only slightly more than the regular 95 RON octane fuel that is widely available. The quality of fuel also varies slightly from country to country, so the CR may need to be adjusted to compensate in some instances. Be prepared to reduce the CR if it proves to be too high, or consider increasing CR if it can be usefully increased.

With 90-91 octane fuel, consider 9:1 compression to be the maximum. If a reduction in CR needs to be made consider 8.7:1 to be the lowest to use. Many A-Series engines have 8.3 or 8.5:1 CR as standard. Increasing the CR from these low levels always results in an increase in engine torque

provided the increased compression is able to be tolerated by the fuel being used (octane rating).

With 95-97 octane unleaded fuels, consider 9.5:1 to 10.3:1 to be the maximum CR able to be used on the road. This may seem very high, and too high in the eyes of many enthusiasts, but only for the regular 95 octane fuel that is available. In most instances, however, it won't be too high, and the engine's overall performance will be better. Essentially, you should aim to get the compression ration as high as you can within the limitations suggested.

If, under acceleration loading, 'pinking' ('pinging') occurs, this indicates that the CR is too high, or the ignition is advancing too quickly. When this happens the engine will not accelerate well and will puff out blue smoke (oil smoke) from the exhaust pipe when the engine is 'pinking.' If, for example, an engine 'pinks' at 3500rpm and above in top gear and

there is no more than 35 degrees of ignition advance the engine has too much compression or a lean fuel mixture. **Caution!** - If the engine has a 5% CO exhaust gas analysed fuel mixture and it 'pinks,' the CR is just too high.

Optimum CR is very important because it will give the engine more 'snap' when it's accelerated, but there are limits. The full list of approximate CR in relation to fuel octane rating is as follows:

8.7:1 - 9:1 with 90 octane fuel
9:1 - 9.3:1 with 91 octane fuel
9.3:1 - 10.8:1 with 95 octane fuel

Compression ratio can be altered by swapping the head for another type as there is a variation in the combustion chamber volumes of the standard factory made cylinder heads. Planing cylinder heads further reduces combustion chamber volume. The benefits of planing the cylinder head to increase the compression are well worthwhile provided the increase in CR is sensible. The engine will deliver better miles to the gallon because of the increased compression, better engine torque and will have more 'get up and go.'

In many instances changing the original standard cylinder head for an alternative type standard cylinder head can result in an increase in compression of a full unit (9:1 to 10:1). For example, fitting a 1300 MG Metro or 1300 MG Metro Turbo head on a 1098cc engine which previously had a standard 26.1cc combustion chambered cylinder head on it will increase CR from 8.5:1 to approximately 9.5:1. If the 1300 MG Metro cylinder head is also planed by 0.035in/0.80mm the CR is further increased to approximately 10.3:1. This is because the standard 1300 MG Metro has a combustion chamber volume of approximately 21.4cc and the removal of 0.012in/0.30mm from the cylinder head gasket face reduces the volume by approximately 1cc. The removal of 0.035in/0.9mm reduces the combustion chamber volume of this particular cylinder head by approximately 3cc to a total of approximately 18.5cc. These figures are approximations only because valves sink further into combustion chambers when they are reground and cylinder head gasket thicknesses vary from manufacturer to manufacturer.

When it comes to all of the common standard engines there are four basic cylinder heads:

• All 850cc, all non-A-Plus 998cc (except Cooper) and all A-Plus 998cc heads have 24.5cc combustion chambers, 1.100in/27.9mm diameter inlet valves and 1.000in/25.4mm diameter exhaust valves. Any variation of original CR was achieved through using pistons with different crowns. The pistons used are either flat-topped or dished (there being two depths of dish). These cylinder heads have round inlet ports 0.950in/24.1mm in diameter.

• All 1098cc engines have 26.2cc combustion chambers, 1.156in/ 29.4mm diameter inlet valves and 1.000in/25.4mm exhaust valves (used with dished top pistons). These heads are rare these days, as are the 997cc Cooper versions of this valve sized cylinder head.

• All 1098cc MG 1100, Riley Kestral 1100, Wolseley 1100, Vanden Plas 1100, MG Midget 1100, Austin-Healey Sprite 1100 and 998cc Mini Coopers used cylinder heads which had 28.2cc combustion chambers, 1.200in/30.5mm diameter inlet valves and 1.000in/25.4mm diameter exhaust valves. The 998 Mini Cooper engine was fitted with a raised-top pistons, while all the 1098cc engines listed here used flat-top pistons. The raised-top 998cc engines piston is no longer readily available in replacement sizes, but flat-topped pistons are. This is the large valve cylinder head commonly referred to as the '295 cylinder head' because of its casting number.

• All 1275cc cylinder heads have 21.4cc combustion chambers. Over the years there have been several versions of this cylinder head which was originally made for '11 stud' MkI Cooper 'S' engines (970cc, 1071cc and 1275cc). Only the MkI and MkII Cooper 'S' cars had these large exhaust valve cylinder heads fitted. These cylinder heads originally had 1.406in/35.7mm diameter inlet valves and 1.219in/30.9mm exhaust valves but frequently suffered from cracking between the valves seats. The factory responded to this problem by reducing the exhaust valve size to 1.156in/ 29.3mm which cured the problem (MkIII Mini Cooper S engines).

With the advent of the standard production 1275cc engine (1967), the valve sizes used were 1.312in/33.3mm for the inlets and 1.156in/29.3mm for exhausts. Later 1275cc engines (1968) in cars like 1300 Riley Kestrals, Austin 1300 GTs and MG 1300s were fitted with cylinder heads which had 1.406in/35.7mm inlet valves and 1.156in/29.3mm inlet valves. It was this valve sized cylinder head that was fitted to MkIII Mini Cooper S engines a few years later.

With the advent of the A+ A-Series engine in the early 1980s there were three versions of the 1275cc cylinder head. The standard 1275cc engine's head which had 1.312in/33.3mm inlet valves and 1.156in/29.3mm exhaust valves. The 1300 MG Metro Turbo which also had 1.312in/33.3mm inlet valves and 1.156in/29.3mm exhaust valves but with much larger inlet ports, better cast combustion chambers and better machined valve seats. The 1300 MG Metro cylinder head which had 1.406in/35.7mm inlet valves and 1.156in/29.3mm exhaust valves, nicely cast combustion chambers and nicely machined valves seats and valve throats. There were two basic cylinder head castings for these A-Plus heads, one with a machined flat surface by the water outlet and the other with an as cast surface in the same area.

CALCULATING & ALTERING COMPRESSION RATIO

If you know the swept volume (displacement) of a single cylinder (bore x stroke) or, in the case of a four cylinder engine a quarter of the total capacity, the volume of an individual combustion chamber plus the volume of any unswept area of the cylinder above the piston and the area created by the head gasket, you can calculate CR.

As an example, original standard 850cc engines had 8.3:1 compression because each cylinder had 212.5cc of capacity (bore x stroke) and 29cc of combustion chamber volume (including the volume of the dish in the top of the piston, the area between the top of the piston and the top of the cylinder and the volume created by the cylinder head gasket). Remember, it is not just the volume of the combustion chamber in the cylinder head that has to be taken into account when compression ratios are worked out: this applies to all engines. Therefore, in our example 212.5cc + 29cc = 241.5cc of total uncompressed volume which gets squashed into just 29cc of space when the piston's at the top of its stroke. This means that dividing the total volume of 241.5cc by 29cc will give us the compression ratio of 8.327 (i.e.: under compression 8.327 units of volume are squashed into the space occupied by a single unit in uncompressed state).

To take our example further, planing the standard 850cc cylinder head by the maximum recommended amount of 0.080in/2.0mm will result in a reduction of the combustion chamber volume from 24.5cc to 19.5cc, a reduction of 5cc. Subtracting 5cc from the standard unswept volume of 29cc gives a new total unswept volume of 24cc. The swept volume (displacement) remains unchanged at 212.5cc so adding the new unswept volume of 24cc (= 236.5cc) and then dividing by 24cc gives a new CR of 9.85:1. This means that on average for every 0.016in/0.4mm of material planed from the gasket surface of an 850cc/998cc cylinder head the combustion chamber volume reduces by 1cc.

Caution! - No more than 0.080inch/2.0mm can be removed

from any 850cc, 998cc, 1098cc or '295' casting number cylinder head.

It's possible to get most models of A-Series engine up to 10.0:1 CR, or more, by planing the cylinder head by the amount required.

To find out what compression ratio an original engine has, write down the engine numbers on the tag riveted to the top of the block's deck at the front of the unit and ask an Austin/Rover dealer to look up the CR.

1275cc head on 850cc engine

Fitting a standard 1275cc engine's cylinder head (21.4cc combustion chamber volume) to an 850cc engine results in a new total combustion chamber volume of 25.9cc (that's 29cc minus the difference in combustion chamber volume of 3.1cc). This results in a compression ratio of approximately 9.2:1 (212.5 + 25.9 = 238.4cc divided by 25.9 = 9.204). Fitting a '295' casting cylinder head which has been planed 0.080in/2.0mm (that's 28.2cc down to 23.2cc) results in a total compression volume of 27.7cc and an increase in compression to 8.67:1.

998cc, 1275cc or '295' head on 998cc engine

With 998cc engines it is a little bit different in that there have been several standard compression ratios even though the same 24.5cc combustion chamber volume standard cylinder head has been used in each case. 998cc engines were available with 8.3:1, 9.6:1 and 10.3:1 compression ratios. Piston dish depth (volume) made the difference between the 9.6:1 and the 8.3:1 CR engines, while the 10.3:1 CR engine had flat-top pistons. The standard 8.3:1 engine has a total compression volume of 34cc, the 9.6:1 engine 30cc and the 10.3:1 engine 27cc (the latter CR

being sufficiently high for use with 95 octane fuel). Planing a standard 998cc cylinder head by 0.080in/2.0mm will result in a reduction in the combustion chamber volume of about 5cc and an increase in CR to approximately 9.6:1 (from 8.3:1). You'll see from this that every 0.016in/0.4mm planed from the head's gasket face will reduce combustion chamber volume by 1cc which can be deducted from the total compression volume given earlier to calculate a new CR in conjunction with the swept volume of 249.5cc (998cc divided by 4). Planing of a 998cc engine's cylinder head (with standard CR of 9.6:1) by 0.048in/1.22mm (3cc) results in a reduction in the total combustion volume to about 27cc and increases CR to about 10.2:1.

A standard '295' casting cylinder head will give total compression volumes of 37.7 (8.3:1 CR), 33.7 (9.6:1 CR) and 30.7cc (10.3:1) in conjunction with the 998cc block. Planed 0.080in/2.0mm (combustion chamber volume reduced from 28.2cc to 23.2cc) the '295' head will give the following compression ratios when fitted to the 998cc block with its three different CRs. The 8.3:1 engine will become 8.6:1 (total compression volume reduced to 32.7cc, the 9.6:1 engine will become 9.7:1 (total combustion volume reduced to 28.7cc) and the 10.3:1 of the flat-top piston engine will become 10.7:1 (total compression volume reduced to 25.7cc).

Fitting a standard 1275cc cylinder head to any 998cc block results in an automatic reduction in total compression volume of 3.1cc. On a 8.3:1 CR engine this results in an increase in to approximately 9.1:1 (total compression volume down from 34cc to 30.9cc), on a 9.6:1 engine an increase in compression to approximately 10.3:1 (total compression volume down from 30cc to 26.9cc) and on a 10.3:1 engine an increase to approximately 11.4:1 (total compression volume down from 27cc to 23.9cc). The latter is getting a bit much for 95 octane fuel, but they seem to run quite well in spite of this factor (use the thickest cylinder head gasket you can find).

1098cc, 1275 or '295' head on 1098cc engine

The standard single carburettor 1098cc engine as found in some Minis has dish-top pistons and an 8.5:1 compression ratio. Total combustion volume is 36.5cc, of which the standard 1098cc cylinder head combustion chamber volume is 26.1cc (similar head to early 997cc engine's). Planing the standard cylinder head by 0.040in/1.0mm results in a reduction in the combustion chamber volume of about 3cc (combustion chamber down from 26.1cc to 23.1cc) and reduction in the total combustion volume to 33.5cc, increasing compression to approximately 9.2:1. Planing the 1098cc head by the maximum recommended amount of 0.080in/2.0mm results in a reduction in the combustion chamber volume of approximately 5cc (combustion chamber volume down from 26.1cc to 21.1cc) and a reduction in the total combustion volume to 31.5cc; CR is increased to approximately 9.7:1.

Fitting a '295' casting cylinder head which has been planed the maximum recommended amount of 0.080in/2.0mm will have a combustion chamber volume of approximately 23.2cc (reduced from 28.2cc) and a total combustion volume of 33.7cc and a CR of about 9.1:1.

Fitting a 1275cc cylinder head (21.4cc combustion chamber volume) to an 8.5:1 compression 1098cc engine results in an engine which has 9.6:1 compression. This results from the 4.7cc reduction in the combustion chamber volume (down from 26.1cc to 21.4cc) and reduction in the total combustion volume from 36.5cc down to 31.8cc.

A flat-top piston (or, more correctly, a minimum-dished top piston) 1098cc engine (older unit from a Riley Kestral or MG 1100 for example) which has a '295' casting cylinder head on it as standard equipment can have the head planed 0.080in/2.0mm which will reduce the combustion chamber volume to 23.2cc (from 28.2cc) and reduce the total combustion volume from 34.6cc to about 29.5cc: CR will increase to approximately 10.3:1.

1275cc head on 1275cc engine

1275cc engines (Mini and Metro) have had a range of compression ratios: 8.0:1 (some economy models), 9.4:1 for MG Metro Turbo engines, 9.4:1 and 9.75:1 for many standard engines as well as 10.1:1 for Cooper engines and 10.5:1 for 1300 MG Metros.

The 8.0:1 CR 1275cc engine had a total compression volume of 49cc. CR can be increased by planing the cylinder head by 0.080in/2.0mm

which will decrease the combustion chamber volume by about 6cc (21.4cc down to 15.4cc) and reduce the total compression volume to 43cc. CR will increase to approximately 9.0:1. The maximum a 1275cc engine's cylinder head can be planed in this instance is 0.100in/2.5mm which will result in a total compression volume of 41cc and a 9.4:1 CR.

The standard 9.4:1 CR 1275cc engine has a total combustion chamber volume of 41cc and planing the head by 0.060in/1.5mm reduces the combustion chamber volume by 5cc, making the total combustion volume 36cc. The compression ratio then becomes 10.5:1.

The 9.75:1 CR 1275cc engine has a total combustion volume of 39cc and planing the cylinder had by 0.040in/1.0mm results in a reduction in combustion chamber capacity of 3cc (that's 21.4cc down to about 18.4cc). With the 39cc of total combustion volume reduced to 36cc, CR increases to about 10.5:1.

The 10:1 CR 1275cc engine has a total combustion volume of 38cc. Planing the cylinder head by 0.025in/0.6mm reduces the volume of the combustion chamber by 2cc and the total combustion volume becomes 36cc. CR is increased to 10.5:1.

The 10.5:1 CR 1300 MG Metro engine has a total combustion volume of 36cc of which 21.4cc is combustion chamber volume. This is enough CR for 95 octane fuel.

Chapter 8

SU carburettors

SU carburettors, and especially single SUs, are largely underrated for road use: in fact they're excellent for this purpose, if not unbeatable.

There are several reasons for using a single SU and the first is that they have been fitted as standard equipment to most of the engines covered in this book, so the throttle linkage is already there as is an acceptable air cleaning system. The advantage of using a single SU is that there are no synchronisation problems and one carburettor is more than capable for flowing sufficient fuel and air for all road going engines modified as described in this book.

A single 1¹/₂in SU is suitable for all 850cc, 998cc and 1098cc engines, and the 1³/₄in SU is suitable for any 1275cc engine. These are the best carburettors for all round general use. Fitting a 1³/₄in SU to an 850cc, 998cc or 1098cc engine is quite possible, but not recommended (although the engine will go very well if correctly

jetted, the all round performance is usually not quite as good as that given by a correctly jetted 1¹/₂in SU). Fitting a 1¹/₂in SU to a 1275cc engine is possible, but will result in a slight reduction in top end power in some instances compared to a 1³/₄in SU.

INLET MANIFOLD

If a tubular exhaust manifold (which is the recommended way to go) is going to be fitted, the best and cheapest way to obtain a stand alone inlet manifold that takes either a 1¹/₂in or a 1³/₄in SU is to buy one from a 1300 MG Metro or 1300 MG Metro turbo engine from a scrapyard. These aluminium inlet manifolds are just excellent and bolt on with sufficient clearance for any tubular exhaust manifold (the centre pipe being the important one here). Aluminium inlet manifolds are also available from Mini specialists new or, sometimes, secondhand. These inlet manifolds are readily available at reasonable prices.

1¾in HIF SU carburettor.

A 1¹/₂in HIF SU or a 1³/₄in HIF SU carburettor will bolt directly onto one of these aluminium inlet manifolds (both carburettors have the same four stud fixing), while one of the earlier two bolt SU carburettors will bolt on after two studs have been removed. You'll also need the original two bolt spacer from the standard cast iron inlet/exhaust manifold combination.

It's quite possible that the aluminium inlet manifold may have to be relieved in one or two places to give the required throttle arm clearance. This factor will soon become apparent if reworking is required because the throttle arm will not be able to be moved through its full arc of travel without fouling the inlet manifold.

The thickness of the inlet manifold (where the stud holes are) is 3/8inch/9.6mm. This thickness and that of the steel plates of a tubular exhaust manifold must be the same if the combination is to pull up tightly against the cylinder head. The washers must also fit the recess of the inlet manifold correctly.

The cast iron inlet/single outlet exhaust manifold as found on all standard single carburettor 998cc/1098cc/1275cc engines is okay for very moderately tuned engines. Note that the cast iron inlet/exhaust set-up can be separated quite successfully, though the exhaust manifold is destroyed in the process. This of course does not matter as you only want the inlet manifold anyway. The standard cast iron inlet manifold flows as well as many of the other aluminium inlet manifolds that are available and is generally quite underrated. While the inlet manifold can be separated from the exhaust manifold section of the combination, the procedure is beyond the scope of this book, though you could get any competent mechanic to do it for you using a disc grinder. You should be aware that there are alignment problems with the cast iron inlet manifold which loses its alignment peg holes when separated from the exhaust manifold.

CARBURETTOR TUNING

The needle in an SU carburettor plays a fundamentally important role in the carburettor's fuel supply characteristics (jetting). Standard SU needles for the 998cc, 1098cc and 1275cc A-Series engines may not be exactly right for your particular engine, although most engines will respond well to the use of

This small hole in the butterfly of a 1½in SU may have to be soldered over to reduce the amount of air going into the engine at idle (to keep idle speed down).

Howley inlet manifold with 1¾in SU. A 1½in SU can be fitted to the same manifold.

well chosen standard SU needles. If no standard needle works well in all areas of the engine's rpm range, the only alternative is to tailor-make a needle to suit, though the procedure for this is beyond the scope of this book. There is another book in the SpeedPro series which deals in great detail with tuning and modifying SU carburettors, it's called *How To Build & Power Tune SU Carburettors* and is also by Des Hammill. This book covers in detail

all aspects of SU carburettor tuning particularly with regard to tuning for individual applications by reprofiling needles.

Bear in mind that in terms of carburation there is no state of tune on any size of A-Series engine that cannot be catered for with needle changes. If an engine does not run from idle through to maximum rpm smoothly and cleanly with no flat spots there's something wrong with the jetting/fuelling/needle (all other factors correct). Always check the SU carburettor float level adjustment: incorrect setting will result in less than best engine performance.

SU needles and parts are available from Burlen Fuel Systems Ltd, Spitfire House, Castle Road, Salisbury, Wiltshire SP1 3SA, England. Tel: 01722 412500, Fax: 01722 334221. This company is the supplier and manufacturer of all genuine SU parts as it is the official licensee.

1275cc engines

The standard needles listed for this engine with a single 1³/₄in SU in the SU Reference Catalogue are BAU, BCH, BEJ, BDL, BFY, BER, BCZ and BFZ. A 4.5 ounce (red) piston spring is also specified for early carburettors with side-mounted fuel bowls (SU part number AUC 4387) and later HIF units with integral fuel bowls (SU part number AUD 4355). This is quite a range of needles and thereby overall jetting. The richest overall mixture is supplied by the DBL needle and this is the needle to try first on any 1275cc engine modified as described here.

SU do not make a huge range of needles suitable for tuned 1275cc engines equipped with a single SU. The BDL is the baseline needle to try first and from which the air/fuel richness factor is increased. The next needle to try is the BBW followed by the BEU and then the BCF.

Retaining the standard air cleaner system is very acceptable, but always make sure that the air filter is serviceable. Always replace the filter element at the standard factory recommended intervals.

The shield plate that is fitted to the inlet manifold when an HIF SU is fitted must always be left in place. This plate shields the base of the carburettor, more specifically the fuel bowl, from

exhaust pipe heat. Further action can be taken to shield the base of the carburettor from heat by getting about three or four 6 or 7 inch diameter tin foil pie dishes and forming them around the base of the carburettor. A plastic tie can also be wrapped around the foil dishes to secure them. This heat shielding is important to keep the fuel as cool as possible.

Any earlier type of carburettor (non HIF) used can have the side mounted fuel bowl wrapped with tin foil dishes to keep the fuel bowl and its contents as cool as possible.

850cc, 998cc and 1098cc engines

The standard SU carburettors for these three engines came fitted with a wide range of 'floating' type needles. Later production versions of these engines were fitted with a single 1¹/₂in or 38mm HIF SU carburettor and the HIF is definitely the best carburettor to use and is easy to obtain. Use the standard 4.5oz (red) piston spring (SU part number AUD 4355). 1098cc engines used ADS, AAY, ABP, ABN and ABJ needles. 998cc engines used ABX, AAG and ABJ needles. The ABJ is the richest needle of these standard needles and is recommended as the first needle (followed by ABD, AAA, AAM and ABY in that order) to try for 850cc, 998cc and 1098cc engines modified as described in this book.

If you decide to use a 1³/₄in HIF SU and inlet manifold (from a 1300 MG Metro, for example) on an 850cc, 998cc or 1098cc engine, the combination will work. The needle to fit in the first place is the BDL (all three engines) and adjust the main jet so that the engine has a suitable idle mixture. The next needle to try, for increased mid-range and top end richness, is the BBW and then the BEU.

Note that HIF SU carburettors

have an idle bypass circuit and on some modified engines this will cause the engine to run too fast at idle. The solution is to blank off the passageway that goes to the downstream side of the butterfly by first removing the small aluminium plug from the hole. Then, with some locking agent applied to the plug, push it back into the hole sufficiently far to block the hole that goes to the throttle bore. Engine idle is then effected by butterfly opening only.

The heat shielding of float bowls is generally required for all engines except, perhaps, in cold countries or in winter. Some engines are not factory fitted with good shields or, sometimes, any shields at all. Lack of heat shielding can lead to fuel expansion problems as heat is radiated from the exhaust manifold which is directly under the carburettor fuel bowl. Expansion causes fuel to run out of the main jet and into the inlet manifold which can cause 'flooding' and make hot starts difficult. Large tin foil pie dishes (3 or 4) are the quick fix to this problem: fitted aluminium shields being the neatest and most professional option.

One possible problem that can arise after the efficiency of the engine has been improved through increasing the spark advance and fitting a 'better' cylinder head, is that the engine can have a misfire at idle. The cause of this is excessive spark advance due to the fact that the vacuum advance mechanism is fully advanced.

When an engine's ignition timing is set, the vacuum advance pipe is always disconnected. The ignition is then set with a strobe light against the relevant crankshaft pulley or damper markings. When the vacuum advance pipe is re-connected, the ignition will be advanced by as much as 3-5 degrees on a standard Mini engine. What can happen on a modified engine is that the amount of vacuum generated can be much higher than on a standard engine and, depending on the calibration of the vacuum advance for the particular distributor, lead to up to 15 degrees of extra advance being realised at idle.

With the butterfly virtually completely shut, and the engine idling at about 800-900rpm, the full amount of vacuum being generated is being taken off the 'downstream' side (vacuum) of the butterfly. This is due to the close proximity of the edge of the butterfly to the small hole that is drilled in the body of the carburettor for vacuum take off.

The solution to this problem is to prevent the vacuum take off hole from getting any inlet manifold vacuum when the butterfly is in the near closed position. The quickest way to do this is to chamfer the edge of the butterfly on the 'up stream' side of the carburettor, adjacent to the vacuum take off hole in the throttle bore of the carburettor. SU butterflies are made out of sheet brass 0.059in/1.5mm thick, and the edge of the butterfly will need to be reduced by 60% adjacent to the vacuum take off hole. The engine will then idle with zero vacuum going into the vacuum canister of the distributor.

This work can be done quite successfully with a small flat needle file and a steady hand. The carburettor will have to be removed from the engine and partially stripped to allow access to the edge of the butterfly, but it doesn't take all that long. The file has to be inserted through the body of the carburettor where the vacuum chamber would normally be screwed down onto the body of the carburettor. It should take about 3-5 minutes to carefully file the edge of the butterfly correctly.

Chapter 9
Exhaust manifold & exhaust system

EXHAUST MANIFOLD

All A-Series engines respond to the fitting of a tubular exhaust manifold and related exhaust system. An aftermarket down pipe system from the exhaust manifold to the underside of the car is available. The rest of the exhaust system is as per the usual aftermarket type. This system is as good as anything else on a road car.

The usual exhaust system fitted to the Mini has a single outlet pipe on the cast iron inlet/exhaust manifold combination which works well for the standard engine but is restrictive for high performance applications. The main advantage of the standard original equipment exhaust system is that it is reliable and relatively easy to replace.

There are several similar tubular exhaust manifolds on the market and most of them follow the same design principle and all work well. The design that prevails these days has the pipe configuration shown in the

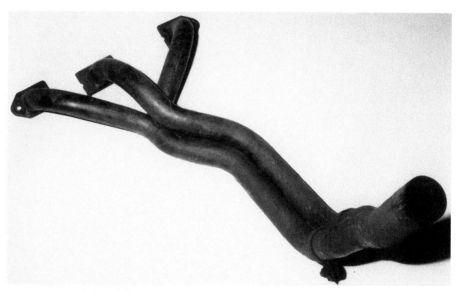

Typical 3-into-2-into-1 tubular exhaust manifold configuration.

accompanying photo and is suitable for all road going engines. These systems are not expensive, and they're reasonably long lasting too. There are a few variations of the same sort of configuration, with some having shorter primary pipes. There are also

three into one exhaust manifolds. The early original equipment three into one exhaust manifold was very good for small bore road going engines, but is hard to come by these days.

In the ideal tubular manifold the two outer primary pipes are of 1.375in/

Short primary-piped 3-into-1 tubular exhaust manifold.

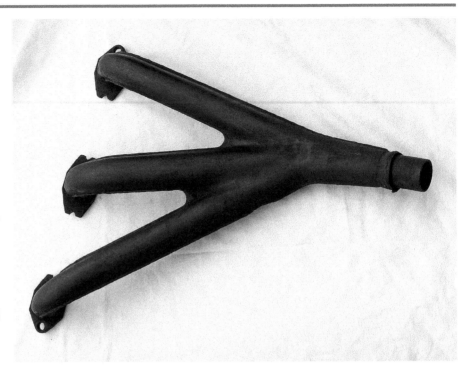

35mm outside diameter and are approximately 11in/280mm long to the bifurcation joint and the 1.5in/38mm outside diameter secondary pipe which is approximately 15in/380mm long. The centre pipe is 1.5in/38mm in outside diameter and is approximately 23in/580mm long. These two 1.5in/38mm outside diameter pipes join side by side and go into a 1.875in/48mm or 2in/51mm outside diameter main pipe underneath the car after making the turn from the engine compartment.

There are larger diameter tubular exhaust manifolds available, but they're not normally necessary for road going engines and are more expensive. They are not necessarily detrimental to power production however, so if you find one secondhand at a reasonable price and in good condition buy it and fit it.

EXHAUST SYSTEM

The ideal main exhaust pipe system for any Mini is the RC40, or equivalent, which uses twin silencers (mufflers). An advantage is that there is no doubt that this system is completely road/street legal when it comes to decibel noise readings and is also very efficient. The Cooper 'S' design of exhaust system, which comprises a 2in/51mm main pipe and a single straight through silencer is also efficient, but the problem is that it's not as quiet as the two box (muffler) RC40 system.

Many enthusiasts don't mind the noise from the Cooper S exhaust type exhaust system, but on a long trip these exhaust systems can become wearing. Consider the RC40 exhaust system, or equivalent, to be unbeatable for road use.

On the road the 850cc, 998cc and 1098cc engines all respond well to a 1.75in/44.5mm outside diameter exhaust main pipe, while 1275cc engines benefit from a 2in/51mm exhaust pipe. While the two box RC40 system is quiet, it's slightly restrictive compared to a system with the first exhaust box removed.

On a high-powered engine, 80bhp and above, the twin box RC40 exhaust system will cause a power loss under wide open throttle use, which can only be cured by removing the first box. For all normal road going use, legal noise levels need to be observed, and the two boxes need to remain in place. However, for weekend racing or track day use the first box needs to be removed. This is usually done by changing the rear section of the exhaust system (two partial exhaust systems are needed for a quick changeover).

Chapter 10

Clutch

There are two types of clutch system employed on transverse engines, they are referred to as 'pre-Verto' and 'Verto.' Both clutch types are completely suitable for road use, although the pre-Verto clutch is dynamically lighter. This means that, although both clutches weigh about the same in total weight, the Verto clutch has more of its weight at the outer diameter of the assembly ,which means that force times distance applies making it effectively the heavier clutch and flywheel. For road use there is no appreciable difference between the two clutches with regard to engine acceleration despite the Verto clutch's greater inertia.

The effectively lighter pre-Verto unit is the less conventional design of the two and it is less easy to change the clutch driven plate (it's on the cylinder block side of the flywheel) with this type. A diagram in this chapter shows the unusual pre-Verto layout (which also applied to an even earlier design

which used coil springs instead of a diaphragm).

Verto clutches are of a conventional looking design, in that all components appear to be on the outboard side of the flywheel. However, both types of clutch have to be completely dismantled to change the driven plate/clutch plate. The standard Verto clutch is certainly less prone to slipping than the lower clamp rated pre-Verto 'brown' or 'light green' cover-equipped clutches, and is generally more trouble-free. The standard Verto clutch is free of clutch slip up to about 70bhp. The MG Metro Turbo clutch cover assembly (meaning the actual diaphragm), for example, is stronger in tension than the standard Verto diaphragm, and all altered 1275cc engines should be fitted with this factory offered uprated/heavy duty type diaphragm cover assembly.

For all general use, stay with the type of clutch your car comes equipped with, as both are good. An

A-Series engine has to be producing quite a lot of power to be able to destroy either type of clutch. On pre-Verto clutches make sure that a suitable pressure diaphragm is fitted.

All pre-Verto diaphragm spring type clutch covers carry a daub of paint on the actual diaphragm spring to indicate their pressure rating. Diaphragms have been marked with light green, dark blue, brown, orange and grey paint to ease identification and, confusingly as diaphragms are neither pressure plates nor clutch/driven plates, are commonly referred to as, for example, 'dark blue plates' or 'orange plates.'

Clamping pressures for the various colour codes are as follows: brown (540Ib), light green (708Ib), dark blue (854Ib), orange (1178Ib) and grey (1280Ib).

For road going 850cc, 998cc and 1098cc Minis the 'light green' or 'dark blue' plates are fine, while for 1275cc units 'dark blue' plates are best.

The solution to clutch plate wear/disintegration on a transverse A-Series engine is to fit a 'cera-metallic' paddle clutch plate. These clutch plates are available from A-Series/Mini specialists for a very reasonable price (given what they do) and once installed can be virtually forgotten about.

850cc, 998 and 1098cc engines modified for road use as described in this book do not usually have problems with the standard clutch. If they do, through unusually hard driving, the solution is to fit a cera-metallic clutch plate and a Unipart 'dark blue' diaphragm clutch cover (as originally fitted to the Cooper 'S') on a pre-Verto clutch assembly, or fit an MG Metro Turbo diaphragm if the clutch is a Verto one. The clutch wrecker is really the 1275cc engine, and a good 1275cc engine can completely wreck a

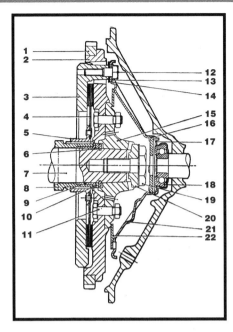

standard component type clutch in less than five minutes.

Anatomy of the pre-Verto diaphragm-type clutch
1 Starter ring gear, 2 Flywheel, 3 Pressure plate, 4 Driven plate, 5 Driven plate hub, 6 Circlip, 7 Crankshaft, 8 Crankshaft primary gear, 9 Primary gear bearing, 10 Thrust washer, 11 Flywheel hub bolt, 12 Driving pin, 13 Lockwasher, 14 Driving strap, 15 Flywheel hub, 16 Thrust plate, 17 Plate retaining spring, 18 Thrust bearing, 19 Flywheel screw, 20 Keyed washer, 21 Cover, 22 Diaphragm spring.
Note the flat attitude of item 22 of the assembled clutch. This factor is vital.

While the manufacturers of cera-metallic clutch plates recommend that a stronger than standard car diaphragm be used in conjunction with their product, this is actually not necessary for road use. **Caution!** - Extra strong diaphragms can be the cause of transmission problems and, ultimately, a ruined engine (crankshaft and block damage). The best diaphragm to use for engines modified as described in this book is a genuine Unipart 'dark blue' diaphragm as originally fitted to the Mini Cooper 'S.' This unit is rated at 854lb of clamp when correctly adjusted. The 'dark blue' diaphragm was made standard on 1.3 Metros so is now readily available as a replacement part. At worst, on a 1275 engine, all that is going to happen is that the clutch is going to slip momentarily as it 'takes up' when let out when the engine is on full throttle. The good thing is that during this time no damage is being done to the clutch system. If an engine is developing over 90bhp, and the clutch slip is noticeable and clearly a problem, then an 'orange plate' will have to be fitted. However, note that thrust washer problems can then become a problem (cause a ruined engine).

The blue daub of paint on the diaphragm indicates which pressure diaphragm the clutch cover should have fitted to it.

Here, the assembled clutch diaphragm is flat, which is the correct attitude for maximum clamping pressure and rapid diaphragm pressure reduction when the clutch pedal is depressed.

Caution! - Not all aftermarket replacement diaphragms are rated at 854lb of clamp. They may look the same and have the same 'dark blue' paint, but they're not necessarily as powerful and could be the cause of clutch slippage, though this problem will usually only show up on a 1275cc engine. Usually any 'dark blue' diaphragm clutch from any manufacturer or remanufacturer will work well for 998cc or 1098cc engines. However, for 1275cc engines the cost of a new Unipart 'dark blue' diaphragm is not excessive and ensures adequate clamping pressure.

Caution! - Do not use a grey or orange diaphragm clutch cover on a road going engine if you can possibly avoid it. They are really quite strong, and can be the cause of almost immediate and ruinous crankshaft thrust washer failure. All clutches need to be set up with the actual diaphragm dead flat when assembled.

CERA-METALLIC CLUTCHES

Cera-metallic clutch plates can be fitted to either type of clutch assembly. One of the most important features of fitting a cera-metallic clutch plate to a pre-Verto clutch assembly is to ensure that the diaphragm is set up correctly so that it has maximum clamp and minimum release pressure. The design of the diaphragm spring means that it is exerting maximum clamp pressure when it is completely flat. This is checked when the flywheel assembly is off the engine by doing a dummy assembly. With the new cera-metallic

Here clutch diaphragm is flat and this is the correct attitude for maximum pressure.

clutch plate fitted to the assembly and everything bolted up, the diaphragm spring is viewed from the side to see how flat it is. If the diaphragm spring is not completely parallel to the flywheel surface, full clamp is not available and, furthermore, when the clutch is disengaged the diaphragm pressure may well increase to the maximum instead of reduce as it should. It's possible to have the diaphragm set so that when the clutch is disengaged the diaphragm spring is flat and at its maximum resistance. This puts a high loading on the crankshaft thrust washers which is very undesirable.

One of the main advantages of using a cera-metallic clutch plate is that they do not seem to wear and this means that the diaphragm shape is optimised for clamping pressure in the almost certain knowledge that everything will remain in optimum condition for a very long time. This is not the case with a standard clutch plate for which the diaphragm has to supply good clamp pressure over a range of heights (clutch plate

thicknesses). The standard clutch plate will change in thickness through wear by as much as 0.050in/1.25mm.

To get the diaphragm spring dead flat may mean having to pack out the diaphragm (using thin flat washers) or having the contact surface of the backing plate machined deeper than standard or machining off the tops of the backing plate lugs. It just depends on the sizes (heights) of the various parts and which way the diaphragm spring is angled when it is dummy assembled. If the diaphragm spring is angled down towards the back of the engine the lugs of the backing plate need to be machined down. If the diaphragm spring is angled away from the back of the engine, it needs to be packed out with thin washers or have the contact surface of the backing plate machined deeper.

Heavy duty standard type clutch plates are available but they cost a similar amount to a cera-metallic clutch plate and offer no advantage except, perhaps, a smoother engagement action. A good 1275cc engine will

literally rip the linings off a standard clutch plate in short order and a new standard clutch kit costs more than twice what a cera-metallic clutch plate costs. Fitting a cera-metallic clutch plate makes good sense financially and mechanically.

The faces that the cera-metallic clutch linings work against on either type of clutch must be in as new condition. This may mean having them remachined (reground preferably). This can often be done in a lathe and may mean that 0.010in/0.25mm will have to be removed from the surfaces to clean them up. The finish has to be as smooth as possible. The flywheel contact face and the pressure plate contact surface can become very scored and worn and this is totally unacceptable.

If the contact surfaces have become heat marked they will not be able to be remachined in a lathe, even if a tungsten carbide turning tool is used. This is because the clutch contact surface has localised hard spots which are as hard as glass. The tungsten turning tool will tend to run up over the hard spots so, while the surface may end up looking better than it was, it will seldom be truly flat and, as a consequence, not acceptable. One solution is to replace the flywheel and pressure plate with alternative ones in good condition (good ones from a scrapyard for example) or buy brand new parts.

If a heat marked flywheel or pressure plate is to be restored the only way to do this is to regrind the surfaces (as opposed to turning them). Some clutch reconditioning shops/machine shops do have suitable equipment, but most don't.

Crankshaft taper in very good condition.

Crankshaft taper in poor condition and no longer serviceable.

In summary

If you're wearing your standard type clutch plate away very quickly, the solution is to fit a cera-metallic paddle clutch. If the clutch is a pre-Verto one, fit a genuine Unipart MkII Cooper S clutch cover/diaphragm. The next aspect is to ensure that the backing plate (pressure plate) is in a good condition and not 'bowed' or scored. Up to 90 bhp/85 foot pounds of torque, a new or good condition secondhand standard backing plate is all that is needed. Don't get into lightening the flywheel or fitting an aftermarket lightweight steel flywheel for road use, as it just isn't necessary. The clutch can remain very standard yet be able to cope with quite a lot of torque/power quite reliably with just a few simple changes. There might be a little bit of 'clutch squeal' on the first few applications, but it's nothing to worry about and no damage is being done.

If your 998cc engine has a Verto clutch, replace the clutch plate with a cera-metalic one and fit a new Verto clutch cover assembly. Consider using an uprated/heavy Verto clutch cover if your engine is a 1275cc one. These clutch covers are available from Mini specialists. Irrespective of which type of clutch you have, use a new clutch cover to ensure that the diaphragm is to specification. Diaphragms tend to lose their tension with age and use. Always fit a new clutch cover when using a cera-metallic clutch plate.

In all cases, the flywheel and the backing plate surfaces which the clutch plate contacts must be flat and smooth. Any items which have 'heat check' marks on them are bowed, and must be replaced or remachined.

The diaphragm must then be reset to compensate (must be dead flat when assembled).

CRANKSHAFT TAPER PROBLEMS

The give-away to a crankshaft taper problem is found when removing the flywheel from the crankshaft to replace the clutch plate. The tapers must lock together when the main bolt is tensioned. If they do, when the factory puller is used to separate the flywheel from the crankshaft taper the two must part with a 'bang.' If they don't, and the flywheel has to be drawn off nearly all of the way, the tapers have fretted' and 'picked up'. Expect damage to the flywheel taper and, to a lesser extent, the crankshaft taper (this is a much tougher material and, as a consequence, is less prone to damage).

Removing a flywheel which won't come off using a conventional puller

This happens much more frequently than you might imagine. Under high tension, the washers under the three bolts distort, and the thread of the central bolt starts to bend, while the flywheel remains firmly fixed to the taper of the crankshaft. The solution is to leave the puller in place, and under as much tension as possible, and apply heat using an oxy-acetylene torch to the hub of the flywheel. The heat, and lots of it, is applied as quickly as possible for the full 360 degrees of the hub so that it expands the hub. For a short time, before the heat has time to transfer into the taper of the crankshaft, the flywheel is momentarily larger than the taper and will part from it.

This may not always work,

however, especially if there is a large amount of fretting. The instant you realise that the flywheel is not going to 'pop off', place a large chisel which has had the sharp edge made blunt in contact with the flywheel hub, about $1/2$in in from the end of the flywheel (that's 90 degrees to the crankshaft axis) and hit hard with a $1/4$ pound lump hammer. The vast majority of difficult to remove flywheels will come off with this treatment.

Warning!/Caution! - Don't try to use a flywheel or crankshaft with a damaged taper, the problem can lead to serious flywheel failure. Damaged tapers mean the flywheel may not run true radially and as it is often at high rpm and has considerable mass this is potentially a disastrous situation. Take no risks with flywheels!

Crankshaft and flywheel taper wear is a problem on many standard 1275 engines. The more modified from standard the 1275cc engine, the more likely it is to have a taper fretting problem, especially if the flywheel has not been fitted as prescribed by the manufacturer. Taper fretting is caused by movement between the taper of the crankshaft and the internal taper of the flywheel. To reduce the prospect of ending up with an unserviceable flywheel and crankshaft, the following needs to be observed. The tapers need to be lapped into each other using 400 grit mould maker's lapping paste, and there must be a 100% contact. The flywheel securing bolt must be tightened to the specified factory torque. The keyplate must fit into the slots in the flywheel and the crankshaft tightly, and the tighter the better (within reason). KAD keyplates do this very well as they are made to the top size of the tolerance. The flywheel retaining bolt must take the torque. Most do but KAD makes a higher quality than standard bolt. Many mechanics don't fit the locking washer preferring to mate the underside of the retaining bolt directly onto the surface of the keyplate, which is fine, the rigidity of the assembly being paramount. Provided the flywheel assembly runs dead true on the crankshaft, is perfectly balanced, and the crankshaft's torsional vibration damper is in a serviceable condition, there will usually be few problems.

The taper fretting problem stems, in the first place, from the fact that, with the engine turning, the flywheel follows it's own orbit accompanied by a gyroscopic effect. To explain this principle, consider a large disc grinder which is turning at high speed. If you try to move the disc grinder quickly, you can't do it (because of the gyroscopic effect) even though the actual disc is quite a light item. A heavy flywheel and clutch assembly, like that of a Mini turning to 7000rpm, for example, has huge interior forces. Secondly, the crankshaft has a bending moment in it, and the higher the rpm, the greater the bending moment. So here we have the flywheel turning in it's orbit at high rpm, and following its path (from which it will not be deviated) and the crankshaft which is bending as it rotates. The result is that the tapers of the flywheel and the crankshaft are tied together but, in part, are not actually doing the same thing. The forces involved are massive and this is what causes the fretting.

When buying an engine, it pays to remove the flywheel and check the condition of the crankshaft taper because, if it's damaged at all, the engine is useless. If possible, find out what the crankshaft taper is like before handing over money! Although flywheels are relatively disposable, because they are easy to replace, the condition of the crankshaft taper is the major issue. In the vast majority of instances, if the flywheel taper is damaged, so is the taper of the crankshaft. But, in many instances, what looks to be damage to the taper of the crankshaft is material that has adhered itself to the taper crankshaft off the flywheel. This can be removed easily (a very fine file used very lightly to file the proud material off) to reveal a taper which is essentially undamaged. Great care is needed to remove the excess material, though, as it's all too easy to start removing material from the crankshaft! The excess material should really be ground off using a cylindrical grinder, but this is a costly exercise.

The crankshaft is steel and the flywheel is made out of cast iron. Cast iron is softer than the steel of the crankshaft and fares worse than the crankshaft. When you fit a steel flywheel the two components are then of similar hardness/toughness, and they deteriorate at about the same rate. The ensuing mess, however, can be considerable, and it's not unknown for it to be impossible to remove flywheels from the crankshaft in one piece.

Chapter 11

Engine assembly & other tips

CYLINDER HEAD FITTING

When alternative cylinder heads are fitted there can be problems with the front of the cylinder head interfering with the top of the water pump housing. This happens when the cylinder head has been planed or the water pump is an aftermarket one with a larger than original housing. If the cylinder head and the water pump are in contact the cylinder head will not pull down onto its gasket properly and the gasket will blow quite quickly, if it seals at all. The solution to this problem is to relieve the relevant area of the head and/or the top edge of the water pump.

The way to check whether or not your cylinder head has clearance is to put the cylinder head on to the top of the block (cylinder head studs in place) without the head gasket in place. This will allow the cylinder head to sit lower than it would with a compressed cylinder head gasket. Visually check to see that the cylinder

head is actually seated fully on the block deck. If it isn't, remove material from head and/or water pump, but (**Caution!**) remember that the cylinder head is only so thick and can have only 0.062in/1.5mm in total removed from the casting in the contact area (use a disc grinder).

CYLINDER HEAD GASKETS

Caution! - All genuine standard Austin/Rover cylinder head gaskets are satisfactory for use on engines with compression ratios that are not too far from standard. This means up to, but not exceeding, approximately 10.5:1. Many engines won't exceed this figure anyway, because of the difficulty of getting the compression up that high, and many engines won't achieve more than 10:1 because of the octane rating of the available fuel. Some original equipment engines have a compression ratio of 10.5:1, of course, and many owners are happy with that. The MG Metro Turbo cylinder head

gasket, which is the type found in more and more standard replacement head gasket sets, will hold 11:1, provided the block's deck and the cylinder head surface is flat and without blemish.

Some aftermarket replacement cylinder head gaskets are not as well made as the genuine original equipment gaskets are and, when these gaskets blow, they almost always blow between the middle cylinders - even on standard low compression engines (8.3:1 and 8.5:1). The reason that these inferior gaskets blow is that they are not reinforced like the better quality original equipment items. This is purely a gasket quality problem: not a cylinder head gasket matching surface or block deck problem. When buying a head gasket always ask whether it is reinforced between the cylinders.

If a good quality cylinder head gasket blows within 1000 miles/ 1600km, or so, of use and the engine's CR is not all that high, such as 9:1,

This cheaper type of cylinder head gasket, which only did 5000 miles/8000km, has blown across the centre portion of the 'flame ring'. This gasket is not a reinforced type. If you ever use a gasket like this, the flame rings must be spray painted with heat resistant paint (VHT or HYCOTE, for example) before they are fitted. That's the area of the flame ring that will face the combustion charge, plus ³⁄₁₆ - ¼in/4-6mm of the surfaces of the gasket around the flame ring (both sides). Do about 5 light coats, letting each coat dry thoroughly. The heat resistant paint tends to increase the life of the cylinder head gasket by a factor of 5.

suspect that the cylinder head gasket matching face and/or the cylinder block deck gasket matching face is not flat. The solution is to have the offending surface remachined by an engine reconditioner/engine machine shop. This is easy enough if the cylinder head is the problem, but not so easy if the block is warped. Block decks can end up out of true at times and, in such cases, the block will have to be machined which means engine out and, usually, a full strip down is required. It is often assumed that if a cylinder head gasket fails the cylinder head could be warped, and that, once the head has been planed all will be well again. While this is largely

Here the bypass hose stub has been ground down and brazed over to block it.

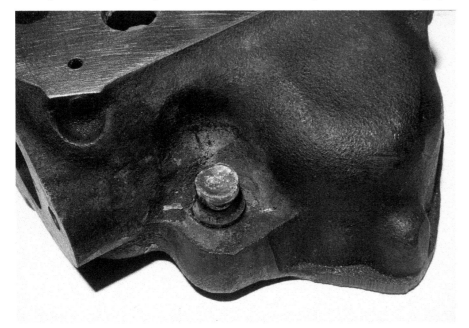

This is a blanking sleeve which is used in place of a thermostat. It evens out the flow of water through the engine, and lowers the operating temperature provided the radiator is of sufficient capacity. Normally, it's a race only item.

true, people rarely consider that the block deck could also be warped. This is probably because the block is regarded as a more rigid structure. However, persistent cylinder head gasket failures can often ultimately be traced to warped cylinder blocks. Any A-series engine stripped down for a rebuild should always have the top of the block cleaned up (surface ground by an engine reconditioner) as a preventative measure against cylinder head gasket failure.

HEAD AND WATER PUMP 'BYPASS HOSE' STUB MODIFICATIONS

Later 1275cc A-Series engines don't have the once standard (and often troublesome) small water pipe connection ('bypass hose') between the underside of the front of the cylinder head and the top of the water pump. If the water pump has an outlet (some don't) but the head you're using doesn't have a matching stub, the stub in the pump will need to be tapped and plugged to block it.

If your pump doesn't have an outlet, but the head does have a stub, the stub can be flattened off a bit (using a disc grinder) and then brazed over to seal it. In the author's experience, doing away with the bypass hose rarely causes any overheating problems.

Always fit a new water pump to an A-Series engine if there is any doubt about the condition of the one on the engine and order one which does not have the small vertically placed outlet.

CRANKCASE VENTILATION

All A-Series engines need adequate crankcase ventilation to prevent engine oil being forced past the rear crankshaft seal. When this happens oil gets on the clutch and it will have to be replaced. Crankcase pressure is a common problem on transverse A-Series engines if certain componentry gets swapped around. Small bore engines have a breather attached to the front tappet chest cover and a breather type rocker cover cap. Additional crankcase breathing can be added by fitting a 1275cc engine's timing chain cover which has a canister on the side of it with a tube connection.

If the engine is being changed over from one gearbox to another, the transfer case can be swapped for one that has provision for crankcase ventilation incorporated into it. Not all transfer cases are drilled for ventilation purposes, although all can be drilled and tapped to provide ventilation. **Caution!** - A transfer case cannot be drilled for ventilation in situ because drilling swarf will get into the oiling system.

Always check to see that the engine's crankcase ventilation system has clear passageways (renew the pipes if necessary) and make sure that there are no restrictive connections that may look large overall but which, in fact, have only small holes in them (1/8in/3.2mm or less). To guarantee adequate engine ventilation an A-Series engine needs at least two 3/8in/10mm inside diameter breather pipes coming off it, plus a breather cap on the rocker cover. The ventilation pipes can go into the air cleaner housing as per standard, or they can go into a separate ventilation bottle.

ENGINE COOLING

Standard engines can be marginal in keeping the water temperature down, particularly once the engine has been altered. The 1275cc engine is the most difficult to keep cool when higher rpm is used and the engine loaded. The only solution is to ease off the throttle.

850cc, 988cc and 1098cc engines are not as prone to overheating because they generate less heat, and because the cooling system is better able to cope with the amount of heat (it's the same basic cooling system). The water pump on the 1275cc engine is turned faster than those on the other engines, to circulate the water a bit quicker, but this still only improves the situation slightly. The cooling problems only tend to start once the compression ratio has been increased to at least 10.0:1. A 1275cc engine which has more than this amount of compression will almost certainly tend to overheat when the engine is fully loaded.

To prevent overheating, all engines must have a radiator that is in excellent condition. A 1275cc engine really needs to be fitted with a new 4 core radiator, and all other engine capacities should be fitted with a new standard replacement radiator.

Make sure that the rubber radiator surround is in good condition (if fitted) and that it seals the gap between the side of the radiator and the wheelarch. This rubber surround is fitted to ensure that the air pushed through the radiator

by the fan actually goes into the wheelarch and away from the car, and is not recirculated as would happen if the rubber was ill-fitted or missing. Making a surround that seals the gap between the rear of the radiator and the inner wing is a worthwhile thing to do if you are experiencing cooling problems.

Fitting two or four spot lamps at the front of the car can also affect the amount of air that goes into the engine compartment, as four spot lamps can effectively block off 40% of the area of the grill.

On some Mini installations, where space allows, making and fitting a shroud between the radiator and the body of the car will prove to be quite beneficial, as it will direct the air that has passed through the radiator core into the wheelarch. Such a shroud can be made out of sheet aluminium (pop riveted together) and can be screwed onto the body of the car with PK screws.

If an engine continues to overheat, the next step would be to fit a 'tropical fan'. This fan is a six-bladed, all metal fan, and was originally fitted to all export cars destined for warm climates. This fan is available new from Mini specialists, or secondhand at car shows and auto-jumbles. While this fan

costs a bit more power to drive than the standard plastic, multi-bladed one, it moves a lot more air and keeps the engine cool. In most instances, this measure is enough to keep the water temperature under control.

As a further safeguard against boiling the water in the engine, add 'Water Wetter' to the water. This will prevent the water boiling at elevated temperatures, and help save the engine from possible damage, but it is not a cure all and has its limitations. For more information on Water Wetter, contact Red Line Synthetic Oil Corporation, 6100 Egret Court, Benica, CA 94510, USA (web: www.redlineoil.com).

Always fit a new thermostat that has been checked for point of opening, and which preferably has a small hole in the surround so that all air can be bled out of the cooling system. A $1/8$in - $3/16$in diameter hole or two can always be drilled in the flat section surround of the thermostat.

Fit a new fan belt, and adjust the tension correctly.

In all cases, ensure that all of the inner wing slots are uncovered. If a car has been fitted with plastic protective under-guards, for example, the wing slots may be covered, and the plastic guards will need to be altered.

www.velocebooks.com/www.veloce.co.uk
All books in print • New books • Special offers • Newsletter

Chapter 12

Gearbox & final drive ratios

CLOSE RATIO GEARBOXES

This is an aspect of Mini tuning that is often bypassed because gearboxes are regarded as being very complicated and one set of gears is pretty much like another set of gears. This is not the case at all. Gearing can be a major factor in getting the most out of the engine. The rate of acceleration can be improved by a considerable margin by fitting a close ratio gearbox and suitable final drive ratio, though top speed will be reduced. When it comes to road use the idea of having the optimum gear ratios as opposed to the standard car's seldom occurs to many.

Any Mini gearbox can have its ratios determined (engine off the gearbox) in about ten to twenty minutes. Once you are acquainted with what actually is what, it's all very simple as the diagrams in this chapter show.

Fitting a close ratio gearbox to an engine modified as suggested in this book may seem to be a bit 'over the

top' but, in fact, it isn't and a good result is possible.

The factory had the close ratio gearbox situation pretty much sorted out as early as 1963 when the first Mini Cooper 'S' cars were introduced. The MkI Cooper 'S' came with 970cc and 1071cc engines in 1963 and 1964 and with gearboxes which had much closer ratios than other Mini models. Optional was a factory fitted very close ratio gearbox, with even closer ratios than the standard fit Mini Cooper 'S' close ratio gearbox.

When the 1275cc MkI Mini Cooper 'S' came out very late in 1964 it, too, had the option of a factory fitted very close ratio gearbox (the 1275cc MkI Mini Cooper S was made between 1964 and 1967). The 'optional' very close ratio gearbox (generally referred to as the 'optional box' nowadays) had three speed synchromesh (2nd, 3rd and 4th) with the following ratios:

1st gear   2.570:1

2nd gear   1.780:1
3rd gear   1.242:1
4th gear   1.000:1

Further, these 'optional gearboxes' could be fitted with a wide range of final drive ratios as follows: 3.765:1, 3.939:1, 4.133:1, 4.267:1 and 4.350:1.

This choice meant that the likely requirements for any application were well and truly covered. Even today many people use these early Cooper S 'optional gearboxes' in competition because they have ideal ratios. Admittedly, these early gearboxes are not as easy to find as they used to be, but they are still around if you look hard enough for them. Most have been broken over the years, which tells you that, over and above normal wear and tear, these gearboxes were not all that strong in the first place.

Note that Special Tuning (BL's competition parts operation) sold straight cut gear sets for racing use between 1963 and 1972. These had the same ratios as the helical gears in the optional gearboxes. Today, Mini Sport offer identical straight cut three and four synchromesh direct replacement gear sets for Mini gearboxes.

Today's aftermarket gearbox industry doesn't really offer better ratios in four speed gearboxes than the factory did in the early 1960s, but it does offer stronger straight cut gear sets for which parts are readily available. As a consequence the aftermarket gearbox industry now caters for anyone wanting close ratio gearboxes for Minis (that's three speed and four speed synchromesh for any model of gearbox). The current list of manufacturers of these types of gear sets includes Jack Knight, Tran-X Gears, Quaife, Mini Sport.

The disadvantage for drivers using an original early optional gearbox is the lack of synchromesh on first gear. Available from the factory for Cooper 'S' cars up until 1967 in remote gear change and three speed synchromesh form only, it was never available as a rod change gearbox or with four speed synchromesh. All Minis had three speed synchromesh gearboxes until 1967, at which point 1st gear was made synchromesh (four speed synchromesh) and the three speed 'optional gearbox' was phased out.

Other factory made gearboxes which had better ratios (although not exactly the same ratios) as those found in standard production road cars were those found in MkI 997cc Mini Coopers from 1961 to 1963 and the MkI 998cc Mini Coopers from 1963 to 1967. This was a three speed synchromesh remote gear change gearbox with the following ratios:

1st gear   3.200:1
2nd gear   1.916:1

3rd gear   1.357:1
4th gear   1.000:1

The MkII 998cc Mini Cooper (1967 to 1970) used the same gear ratios, but the gearbox had four speed synchromesh and it was also a rod change gearbox. This gearbox has the closest ratios of all of the production gearboxes available in four speed synchromesh form. All Mini Coopers (as opposed to Cooper 'S's) were factory fitted with 3.675:1 final drives.

The MkIII Mini Cooper 'S' (1970 to 1972) had four speed synchromesh and a remote gear change until production ceased in 1972. The Mini Clubman 1275 GT (1969 to 1972) had four speed synchromesh and a remote gear change until 1972, then switched to rod change for the rest of the production run which ended in 1981. The standard final drive ratio was 3.765:1 but MkIII Cooper 'S' cars only could be ordered with lower ones (3.939:1, 4.267:1 and 4.350:1) or a higher 3.444:1. The gear ratios for these gearboxes were:

1st gear   3.300:1
2nd gear   2.070:1
3rd gear   1.350:1
4th gear   1.000:1

Other cars which had the same gear ratios as the MkIII Cooper 'S' and 1275 GT gearboxes in four speed synchromesh form were MG 1300 as made from 1968 to 1972, 1300 Riley Kestrel as made between 1968 and 1971 and Austin 1300 GT as made from 1969 to 1973. These gearboxes all had remote gear changes. The Austin 1300 GT was fitted with the same gear ratios but in a rod change gearbox for 1973 and 1974. All of these gearboxes had a 3.650:1 final drive (it suited the 12 inch wheels that these cars used). While most of these

cars have completely disappeared, the engines and gearboxes are often still around and can be fitted to Minis.

CHECKING GEARBOX RATIOS
Checking Mini gearbox ratios is not difficult at all and can be done with the engine in the car in about 30 minutes. The first method is reasonably accurate; certainly accurate enough to identify the ratios with some confidence. However, the more careful you are with the checking procedure, the more accurate the checked results will be.

Determining final drive ratio
The first thing to do is find out what the final drive ratio is. To do this the car must be on level ground, the sparkplugs removed, fourth gear engaged and top dead centre (TDC) marks on the timing chain cover and the rim of the crankshaft damper/pulley clearly marked (white felt tipped pen/daub of white paint). While highlighting the timing marks is a fiddly task, it can be done, especially if the grill has been removed. With the engine at top dead centre (TDC), a front tyre must also be marked with chalk in the six o'clock (hour hand) position.

Push the car gently along (you'll need more than one person) with 4th gear engaged and carefully count the number of engine revolutions and partial revolutions for one complete revolution of the marked front wheel. If the engine turns four complete revolutions exactly, the overall final drive ratio is 4.0:1. If, as is usual, the engine requires a part revolution to complete one revolution of the front wheel, that amount will have to be estimated in one hundredths of a revolution. If the final drive ratio is 4.133:1 or 3.939:1, for instance, it's quite easy to estimate the true ratio as one ratio represents not quite four full revolutions of the engine and in the other slightly less than four.

Estimating whether the final drive ratio is a 3.444:1 or a 3.675:1 is another matter and is a bit more difficult. The solution here is to mark the rim of the crankshaft damper or crankshaft pulley at 90, 180 and 270 degrees as well as TDC: each quadrant then represents 25 one hundredths of a full revolution. The easiest way to measure the amount of partial crankshaft revolution is to temporarily fix a 5in/125mm diameter 360 degree protractor onto the crankshaft damper/pulley nut using plasticine/ BlueTac/chewing gum (as centrally as possible). Put white marks on the edge of the protractor at the four 90 degree points. The way to get the best access to the crankshaft nut and position the protractor is to remove the grill of the car.

It doesn't matter whether 'straight cut drop gears' are fitted to the gearbox or an aftermarket final drive, this method will still give a true indication of the final drive ratio.

Determining gear ratios (method 1)

The next part of the scenario is to find out what the gear ratios are of 1st, 2nd and 3rd gears. This is done by taking the car back to the original position so that the chalk mark on the tyre is in the six o'clock position again. This time 3rd gear is engaged and the revolutions of the engine counted as the front wheel is turned through one full revolution. Repeat this process with 2nd and 1st gears engaged. Get the partial revolution aspect of the crankshaft rotation as accurate as you can as it does affect the results of the calculations you'll have to do.

With the number of full and partial crankshaft revolutions in each of the indirect gears known and the final drive

ratio known, the indirect gear ratios can be worked out by dividing the engine revs by the final drive ratio (do this with a calculator). For example, if the engine has turned approximately 3.7 complete revolutions for one full revolution of the wheel (in 4th gear), the final drive can be identified as 3.765:1. If the engine turns 9.6 times in 1st gear, 6.7 in 2nd and about 4.7 in 3rd, the overall indirect ratios are 2.570:1 (1st), 1.780:1 (2nd) and 1.242:1 (3rd): this means you have the optional close ratio gearbox (or one with the same ratios).

Note that if 'straight cut drop gears' (lower ratio) have been fitted but you don't know it, you can't work out what the true ratios of the gearbox are, but you can work out what the overall gearing of the car is.

Determining gear ratios (method 2)

The second and dead accurate method of determining gear ratios relies on counting teeth and can be used when the gearbox is out of the car and the engine separated from it. All standard Mini four speed gearboxes operate on the same principle. The individual gears (pinions) of all gearboxes are all in the same place, the only difference being the number of teeth on each individual gear. The following method can be applied to any original equipment type Mini gearbox to work out the actual gearbox ratios.

In terms of the number of teeth on individual gears, the gear train example given here is that of the 1963 to 1967 Mini Cooper 'S' three speed synchromesh 'optional gearbox.'

The drive goes from the crankshaft to the idler gear and then to the first motion shaft gear 1 in a vertical path from the crankshaft. The drive from the crankshaft to the first motion shaft is at a ratio of 1:1 on standard

Minis. In the case of all standard Minis the gearbox's 'first motion shaft'/'input shaft' turns at the same speed as the crankshaft. (Although there is no ratio change between crank and first motion shaft on standard Minis, there is if aftermarket 'straight cut drop gear sets' are used. If such a gear set is fitted there is a reduction, and the effective ratios of all gears change as a consequence. This means a further series of calculations must be done to work out what the ratios are.)

The layshaft has 13 teeth on gear 11 on the straight cut (as standard) first gear (the smallest diameter gear on the layshaft), 17 teeth on second gear 10, 20 teeth on third gear 9 and 23 teeth on gear 8 that is driven by the first motion shaft drive gear 2 (gears 1 and 2 are on the same short shaft and, as a consequence, always turn at the same speed).

Although there are four individual gears on the layshaft only three of them are actually gears (first, second and third). The largest of the four gears on the layshaft 8 is actually a driven gear meaning that it is used to transmit drive to the layshaft: it is not fourth gear. 2 and 8 are transfer gears.

The drive from the crankshaft goes to the 'first motion shaft' gear 1. Gear 2 of the 'first motion shaft' which has 22 teeth on it, drives the 23 tooth gear 8 of the layshaft. This means that in our 'optional gearbox' example there is a reduction (0.956:1) in the drive ratio. This figure is arrived at by dividing 22 by 23 (that's dividing 22 gear teeth by 23 gear teeth, a calculation best done on a calculator). All four gears on the layshaft turn at the same shaft speed and so all are subject to this ratio.

Other gearboxes will have different numbers of teeth on these two gears and different reductions accordingly (the standard 998cc engine

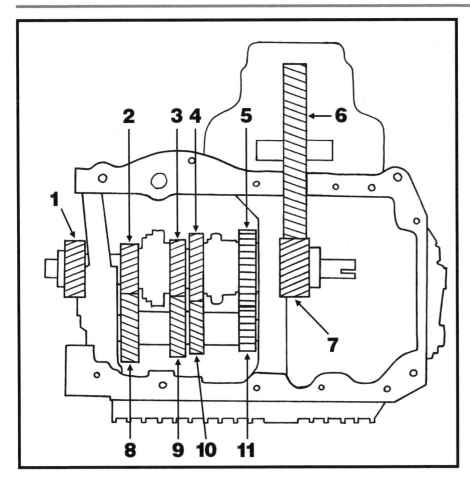

Mini gearbox with the main shaft at the top and the layshaft at the bottom. Each gear is numbered to identify it and its function as described in the text.
Note. Hub A is situated between gears 2 and 3 and hub B is between gears 4 and 5.

gearbox has 17 teeth on gear 2 and 29 or 30 teeth on gear 8, for example).

Moving deeper into the gearbox, the layshaft drives the three indirect gears (that's third gear 9, second gear 10 and first gear 11). All of these forward gears in the gearbox are turning all of the time (called 'constant mesh'). The principle of operation of the gearbox is that the crankshaft turns gear 1 (which automatically turns gear 2 because they are on the same shaft). Gear 2 turns gear 8 (and as the layshaft is a one piece item, all gears on it turn at the same shaft speed). Because of the different gear diameters (different number of teeth on the gears 3 and 9, 4 and 10, 5 and 11) gear numbers 3, 4 and 5 will be turning at different speeds from each other. The engagement of the syncro hub B on gear number 5s drive teeth gives 1st gear or gear number 4s drive teeth gives 2nd gear; while syncro hub A engaging on gear number 3s drive teeth gives 3rd gear or gear number 2s drive teeth gives 4th gear.

The main gear shaft which has gears 1, 2, 3, 4, 5 and 7 on it is comprised of two shafts (first motion shaft and mainshaft). The separation of the two shafts is between 2 and 3. Fourth gear is not actually a gear system like 1st, 2nd and 3rd but is instead a direct drive from the first motion shaft gear 1 straight through to the final drive gear 6 at the far end of the main gear cluster. The drive is straight through from gear 1 to 6 as engaging 4th gear effectively makes

1st gear power transmission path from crankshaft (input gear) to final drive differential unit (and thence to driveshafts).

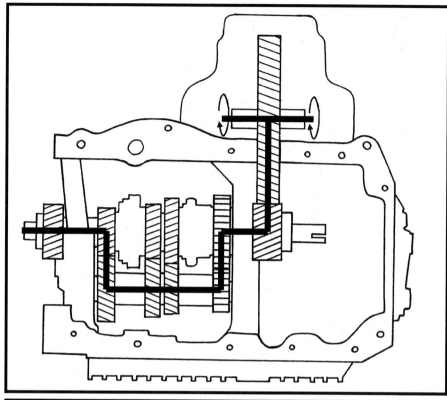

2nd gear power transmission path from crankshaft (1st motion/input shaft gear) to final drive differential unit (and thence to driveshafts and front wheels).

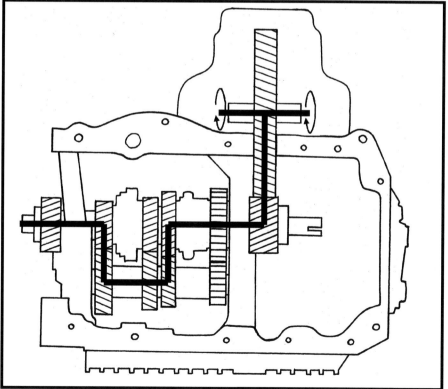

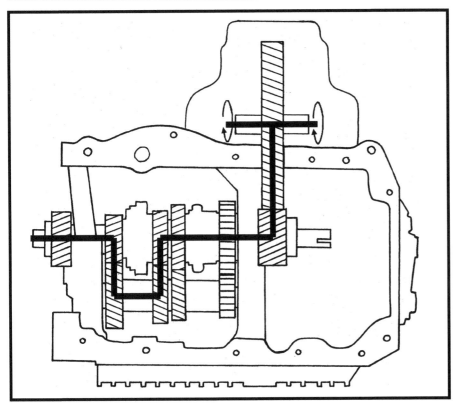

3rd gear power transmission path from crankshaft (1st motion/input shaft gear) to final drive differential unit (and thence to driveshafts and front wheels).

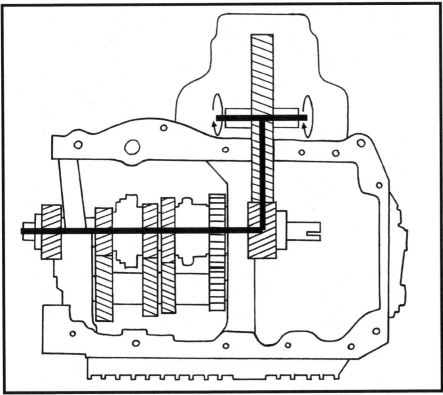

4th gear power transmission path from crankshaft (1st motion/input shaft gear) to final drive differential unit (and thence to driveshafts and front wheels).

The difference between helical gears (top) and straight cut gears.

the split mainshaft a single shaft. When 4th gear is engaged, synchro hub A fitted to the mainshaft between gears 2 and 3 engages the drive teeth on the first motion shaft at gear 2. The drive between 1 and 7 is 1:1. This is how 4th gear is effective. Gear 6 is the final drive.

POSSIBLE GEARBOX AND FINAL DRIVE COMBINATIONS

The optional Cooper 'S' gearbox has it's limitations with regard to fitting high final drive ratios (3.1:1 or 3.2:1). If such a gearbox was fitted with a 3.1:1 or 3.2:1 differential ratio it would be similar to starting off in second gear in a car equipped with a standard ratio gearbox, which is why this type of gearbox always has a low final drive ratio. The 2.570:1 for first gear is quite high compared to a standard late 850cc/998cc gearbox ratio which is 3.650:1 (fitting a 3.444:1 final drive

is about as high as you can go with an optional close ratio gearbox).

In the early 1960s it was possible to order the optional close ratio gearbox fitted with a 3.939:1 final drive for example (4.35:1 was the lowest available). There was no need for 'drop gears' with this gearbox and final drive ratio as it was about as low as things could be, or would need to be, taken.

The overall gearbox reduction (number of turns of the engine crankshaft for every revolution of the front wheels) was - calculated by directly multiplying the gear ratio of each gear by the final drive ratio (no non-1:1 'straight cut drop gears' fitted) - as follows.

1st gear at 2.570 x 3.765 = 9.676:1.
2nd gear at 1.780 x 3.765 = 6.541:1.

3rd gear at 1.242 x 3.765 = 4.676:1.

4th gear at 1.000 x 3.675 = 3.675:1.

This means that there are 9.676 turns of the engine in first gear for each full turn of the front wheels, 6.541 turns of the engine in second gear for each full turn of the front wheels, 4.676 turns of the engine in third gear for each full turn of the front wheels and of course 3.675 turns of the engine in 4th gear for each full turn of the front wheels.

The late 850cc/998cc Mini gearbox, for example, had different gear ratios which were as follows:

1st - 3.525:1
2nd - 2.123:1
3rd - 1.433:1
4th - 1.000:1

With a standard 3.675:1 final drive fitted to such a gearbox the result is an overall gearbox reduction of:

1st gear was 12.954:1
2nd gear was 7.813:1
3rd gear was 5.266:1
4th gear was 3.675:1

This means that there was 12.954 turns of the engine for every full turn of the front wheels in 1st gear, 7.813 turns of the engine for every full turn of the front wheels in 2nd gear, 5.266 turns of the engine for every full turn of the front wheels in 3rd gear and 3.675 turns of the front wheels in 4th gear.

With standard 10 inch wheels and a 3.765 final drive ratio a Mini does 14.70 miles an hour per 1000rpm in top gear. This means that with an engine that revs up to 7000rpm any car fitted with this differential ratio will do 102.29mph, irrespective of what the 1st, 2nd or 3rd gearbox ratios are.

Using the gearbox examples given, the two top gear speeds are identical but the 1st, 2nd and 3rd gear maximum speeds at 7000rpm are quite different. The common factor here is the final drive ratio giving the miles per hour per 1000rpm of the engine, but that's the end of the similarity between the two gearboxes from a practical point of view.

To calculate the speeds possible in each gear in the two different ratio gearboxes, divide 14.70 by the gear ratio. This means dividing 14.70 by 3.525 which equals 4.170 miles per 1000rpm of the engine for the standard ratio 850cc/998cc gearbox.

	CR gbx	Std 850/998cc gbx
All at 1000rpm –		
1st gear		
	5.719mph	4.170mph
2nd gear		
	8.258mph	6.891mph
3rd gear		
	11.835mph	10.258mph
4th gear		
	12.96mph	ditto

These figures multiplied out using the maximum rpm that the engine is revved to result in the following speeds in the gears:

	CR gbx	Std 850/998cc gbx
1st gear		
	40.03mph	29.19mph
2nd gear		
	57.80mph	48.23mph
3rd gear		
	82.84mph	72.51mph
4th gear		
	102.92mph	102.92mph

The following are examples of miles per hour speeds with standard 10 inch diameter wheels fitted to Minis in relation to the various final drive ratios available:

All at 1000rpm –
2.950 (2.9) = 18.28mph
3.105 (3.1) = 17.82mph
3.267 (3.2) = 16.94mph
3.444 (3.4) = 16.07mph
3.647 (3.6) = 15.18mph
3.939 (3.9) = 14.06mph
3.765 (3.7) = 14.70mph
4.133 (4.1) = 13.40mph
4.267 (4.2) = 12.96mph
4.355 (4.3) = 12.71mph

The overall gearbox ratio is altered by changing the final drive ratio to obtain the best spread of ratios for the application. Most people settle on a particular final drive ratio that suits the majority of road work that they are doing. For road going use using an optional close ratio gearbox consider 3.765:1 to be the lowest final drive to use for 850cc and 998cc engines revving to 7500rpm; 3.444:1 for 1098cc engines revving to 6000rpm and 3.444:1 for 1275cc engines revving to 7000rpm

For motorsport use, for example in hill climbing, where the speeds do not really ever get over 100mph consider 3.9:1 to 4.1:1 to be the likely range, while circuit racing gearing will be anything from 3.4:1 down to 3.9:1.

FINAL DRIVE RATIOS

All Mini gearboxes have a similar final drive design, but not all Mini gearboxes have the same final drive ratio. Over the years there has been quite a range of standard final drive ratios available for manual Mini gearboxes. The list is as follows:

2.950:1
3.150:1
3.267:1
3.444:1
3.647:1
3.765:1
3.939:1

4.133:1
4.267:1
4.350:1

The 3.444:1 is one of the most common final drive ratios and is fine for town use with all engines, but it is not ideal for motorway use as the engine will rev too hard at 70mph.

The 3.1:1 final drive (later economy gearbox) is better for motorway use than a 3.444:1, although the hill climbing ability of the engine will not be as good. That said there are not really too many hills that will have a major effect on the progress of a well tuned Mini driving through a 3.1:1 final drive. The 'stronger' the engine, the less effect a 3.1:1 ratio final drive ratio will have on overall vehicle performance. Although a compromise, for all general use the 3.1:1 economy gearbox is excellent.

To work out how fast your Mini will go with a particular final drive ratio, use the following table to calculate the speed by multiplying mph per thousand rpm by the rpm your engine is capable of revving to (happily). The examples given are for 10 inch diameter wheels:

All at 1000rpm –
2.950 (2.9) = 18.28mph
3.105 (3.1) = 17.82mph
3.267 (3.2) = 16.94mph
3.444 (3.4) = 16.07mph
3.647 (3.6) = 15.18mph
3.939 (3.9) = 14.06mph
3.765 (3.7) = 14.70mph
4.133 (4.1) = 13.40mph
4.267 (4.2) = 12.96mph
4.355 (4.3) = 12.71mph

If you are looking for a particular final drive ratio there are two reasonably easy ways to find out exactly what is fitted in a particular gearbox. If the gearbox has been separated from the engine, a tooth count is the best way to determine which final drive is fitted. Mark a tooth with white correction fluid and slowly turn the gear, counting the number of teeth as you go. Do this to the crown wheel and the pinion gears. With the count done and rechecked, divide the number of teeth as counted on the pinion into the number of teeth as counted on the crown wheel, i.e. 59 on the crown wheel divided by 19 on the pinion = 3.105. This is the final drive ratio. Failing this, just count the teeth of each and match them up using the following chart:

Final drive	crownwheel	pinion
4.3	65	15
4.2	64	15
4.1	62	15
3.9	63	16
3.7	64	17
3.6	62	17
3.4	62	18
3.2	61	19
3.1	59	19
2.9	59	20
2.7	58	21

If the engine and gearbox are out of the car but are still bolted together, the way to determine the final drive is to count how many times the engine has to be turned to get a driveshaft to turn once. This means engaging fourth gear, removing the sparkplugs and marking a driveshaft's inner joint with a white marking pen. Now count how many full turns and partial turns of the crankshaft it takes to get the driveshaft to turn a single full revolution. If the crankshaft rotated 3.4 times, then the table of ratios earlier in this section shows that the nearest final drive ratio is 3.444:1 and this must be the final drive fitted to the gearbox in question. Note: this method will not be reliable for gearboxes fitted with aftermarket drop gears giving any ratio other than 1:1.

Note. This method will not be reliable for gearboxes fitted with non 1:1 'drop gears'. That's a few standard factory cars, and cars fitted with aftermarket alternative ratio 'drop gears'.

STRAIGHT CUT DROP GEARS

Almost all standard factory Minis had 1:1 ratio 'drop gears' fitted to them. There were some models which had one tooth less on the gearbox input shaft which meant that the gearbox input shaft was 'under-driven' (the gearbox input shaft turned faster than the crankshaft). For the most part, however, standard Minis/Metros have 1:1 ratio 'drop gears' and the following applies to them.

There is a primary gear on the end of the crankshaft which drives an idler gear which in turn drives the first motion shaft gear on the end of the gearbox (this gear is on the end of the gearbox input shaft/first motion shaft). In effect, these gears 'drop' the crankshaft drive down to the gearbox input shaft: hence the expression 'drop gears.' On a standard gearbox the helical drop gears each have 29 teeth. This means that when the crankshaft turns once so does the input shaft of the gearbox.

Note that all standard Minis have 29 teeth on the primary gear and the gearbox first motion shaft/input shaft gear, but the 1275cc engines have a larger diameter crankshaft 'snout.' 850cc, 998cc and 1098cc engine crankshafts have the same sized crankshaft 'snout', so primary gears are interchangeable on these three engines.

Aftermarket 'straight cut drop gears' offer two features. One is that they can change the ratio between crankshaft and gearbox input shaft from 1:1 to, for example, 1.090:1 (which means that the gearbox input shaft is turning slower than the crankshaft). The second is that 'straight cut' gears, as opposed to 'helical' gears, are slightly more efficient at power transmission, though they're noisier because their teeth are not actually in constant contact.

Early straight cut drop gears came in a set which offered two possible reductions from the standard 1:1. The ratios offered were 1.043:1 and 1.090:1. These drop gears had a choice of two gears that could be fitted to the crankshaft (primary gear), one with 22 teeth and one with 23 teeth, an idler gear and one gearbox input shaft/first motion shaft gear with 24 teeth. The 1.043:1 reduction used the 23 tooth primary gear while the 1.090:1 reduction used the 22 tooth primary gear.

To work out the ratio of non-standard drop gear sets, count the number of teeth on each of the three gears (two primary gears and input shaft gear: not the idler gear). Next, divide the number of teeth on the gearbox input shaft gear by the number of teeth on the crankshaft primary gear. For example, 24 divided by 22 = 1.090, while 24 divided by 23 = 1.043.

The idler gear's number of teeth is immaterial and not part of the calculation as it is only a means of transmitting drive from the drive gear (the primary gear on the crankshaft) to the driven gear (the gear on the end of the gearbox input shaft/first motion shaft).

The standard range of final drive ratios for various Minis has included 3.105:1, 3.267:1, 3.444:1, 3.647:1, 3.765:1, 3.939:1, 4.133:1, 4.267:1 and 4.355:1 using the standard 1:1 ratio drop gears. To work out what the new final drive ratio will be when either 1.043 or 1.090 drop gears are fitted, multiply the final drive by the drop gear ratio. Using a 3.444:1 final drive ratio as an example, multiply it by 1.043 = 3.592. Multiplying 3.444 by 1.090 = 3.753. The accompanying table gives the range of overall final drive reductions when using non-standard drop gears with the standard readily available final drive ratios.

1:1 (Std)	1.043	1.090
3.10	3.23	3.38
3.27	3.41	3.56
3.44	3.58	3.74
3.66	3.81	3.98
3.76	3.89	4.09
3.93	4.19	4.29
4.13	4.30	4.50
4.26	4.44	4.64
4.35	4.53	4.74

This is not actually the end of the matter because the fitting of non-standard drop gears effectively reduces the ratios of all the intermediate gears, in many instances making first gear too low and not worth using. Fitting non-standard drop gears is only a good move if the gearbox is a close ratio one, in which case first gear is still very usable. As an example, if the gearbox is a standard production 850 one with a 3.627:1 first gear, fitting 1.090:1 drop gears will change the first gear ratio to 3.953:1 (so low as to be useless), second would become 2.367:1, third would become 1.539:1 and top gear would be 1.090:1.

The advantage of non-standard drop gears is really as a tuning tool in that the overall ratio of the gearbox can be altered by a small amount reasonably quickly and without taking the gearbox to pieces. Having a close ratio gearbox and a reasonably low final drive fitted to it, and then being able to lower the final drive in two very small increments is the significant factor here. In a pure racing situation, for example, this slight difference can make a difference from one type of track to another in that the overall gearing can be altered slightly to suit a particular track. The alternative being to strip the gearbox and final drive and to change the final drive for one with a different ratio. It could be, for example, that the ratio alteration of a particular set of drop gears means that 2nd and 3rd are absolutely 'spot on' for a particular track where first and fourth don't matter quite so much. Alternatively, 3rd and 4th could be optimised for the conditions where 1st and 2nd don't matter quite so much. The overall ratio change is made without disturbing the final drive and having to get into the gearbox itself.

Chapter 13

Brakes & wheels

This chapter concentrates on the standard drum brake system fitted to most Minis. Be aware of the fact that most Minis have sub-standard braking these days, because not all of the components within the system are in the best possible condition. The all brake drum system-equipped Mini needs frequent attention if maximum possible braking efficiency is to be maintained.

Warning - For your safety and that of other road users, all Minis which are going to have engine power output increased - but which will retain drum brakes - must have the whole braking system thoroughly checked, correctly adjusted and parts replaced where necessary. As a very minimum, the brakes must be returned to the equivalent of original condition.

All Minis made later than 1964 have twin leading shoe front brakes. If your Mini has single leading shoe front brakes, change them for the twin leading shoe type by going to a scrapyard (junkyard) and buying the complete front brakes from a later car.

All replacement brake parts are available at reasonable cost and, although total refurbishment of the braking system will cost some money, the end result will be a car that will stop quite well in most normal braking circumstances. The biggest problem with the original drum brakes is the fact that these cars could not be stopped easily from high speed, especially when going down a long hill. Constant braking from high speed (90mph/145km plus) down a long hill or in a panic stop situation from high speed is generally enough to render the drum brakes close to useless if in anything other than perfect condition.

DRUM BRAKE SYSTEM OVERHAUL, ADJUSTMENT & MAINTENANCE

Given their age and the mileage that most drum braked Minis will have covered by now, the first thing that should be replaced is the master cylinder. Kits are available to repair the original, but what can't be repaired is serious pitting and/or wear of the bore. Re-honing of master cylinder bores can only be taken so far, making the fitting of a brand new master cylinder the best, safest and recommended option. In fact, it's best to avoid repairing a master cylinder if at all possible. Fit a brand new one instead.

All of the wheel cylinders also need to be replaced. These items are quite inexpensive and, realistically, while repair kits are available, it's better to buy six new cylinders which just need bolting into position.

Not always obvious is wear in the connecting mechanism between brake pedal and master cylinder. The clevis pin can wear, as can the clevis pin bore in the brake pedal and master cylinder pushrod. This can all add up to quite a loss in effective master cylinder piston movement as well as having to push the brake pedal further than necessary to remove slop from the linkage before the brakes start to work. Fitting a new brake pedal, clevis pin and master cylinder pushrod solves this problem completely.

Steel brake lines can, and do, corrode. Rigid brake pipes have also been known to fracture, especially when they get old and thinned by corrosion – total brake failure being the result ... Complete replacement of all metal pipes is recommended on the basis of maximum safety. Include the very short pipes (which link the two wheel cylinders) found on the back plates of the two front drums. Replacing all of the metal pipes is not particularly difficult, but to make a neat job of it and to ensure all pipes are correctly clipped will take a few hours. It's a good idea to spray all unions with penetrating oil some hours before you start work and to wire brush away loose rust before attempting to undo unions.

Replacing flexible brake hoses is essential. Old brake hoses (as well as some new ones on occasion) can sometimes be seen to be moving when the brake pedal is depressed and the system put under pressure. Ballooning of the brake hose or hoses (even if barely perceptible) increases the displacement necessary (more pedal movement) to bring the brakes into full operation.

The brake drums also wear and can often be worn to an almost unbelievable extent ... If your car has covered more than 50,000miles/ 80,000km the chances are that the drums will be worn sufficiently to require replacement. Fitting brand new replacement drums is really a requirement unless the drums on the car are in as new condition. Four new drums do not cost all that much.

New standard replacement brake shoes are next, followed by new

hydraulic brake fluid. Brake fluid must be completely changed on an annual basis if maximum efficiency is to be maintained. This might appear to be too frequent, but it isn't. Brake fluid absorbs moisture over time.

The brake shoe adjusters on the back plates (front and rear) seize up easily and quickly, and on older Minis it's quite common to find at least two adjusters not working. 'Rounded off' brake adjusters are a result of this problem. What happens is that the adjuster thread seizes up, then a loose-fitting spanner is used to try to turn the adjuster, a bit of resistance is felt and more leverage is used and then the shoulders of the adjuster get rounded off. The end result is frequently a damaged adjuster which no spanner will get a grip on.

Caution! - Always clean the exposed threads of adjusters before trying to turn them. The instant serious resistance to turning an adjuster is noticed, stop trying to turn it. If you've been using a open ended spanner (crescent wrench) go and buy a proper square brake spanner. Spray penetrating oil on the thread of the adjuster and leave it to soak for at least 10 minutes. The front brake adjusters need to be sprayed from both sides of the backplate with the drums off (**Caution!** - don't get spray on the shoes), while the rear adjusters usually only need to be sprayed from the outside.

If the adjusters will still not move, the only solution is to apply heat using an oxy-acteylene torch (most garages have this sort of equipment). Heating the adjuster is almost always enough to allow it to turn again. There will always be the odd time where the adjuster has become so badly rusted that it is impossible to turn. In such cases the best solution is a replacement plate (can be second-hand).

If the adjuster 'square' is ruined in the process of loosening it, buy a brake adjuster repair kit to resurrect your own brake drum backing plates (contact a Mini specialist for details). All of the brakes shoes must be adjusted correctly. It's not an option to leave one adjuster seized solid, for example, and adjust the rest to get as good a pedal as possible.

The best solution to rounding off the adjuster squares is to weld a hexagon nut to the original adjuster. This is not difficult to do, although the backing plate has to be removed.

Even after the replacement of all of these parts it still does not necessarily mean that your Mini will have first class brakes, there's a bit more to it than that ... **Warning** - hydraulic braking systems must be bled properly (follow workshop manual procedure) to ensure that there is no air in the system: air will give a 'spongy' soft feeling to the pedal action and reduce braking effect substantially.

Warning - The brake shoes on Minis must be adjusted correctly to ensure that the pedal does not travel too far. When the brake pedal travels too far (1in/25mm off the floor is too far) the brake shoes have not been adjusted correctly. To adjust the brake shoes correctly, each wheel needs to be jacked-up in turn. Each (of four) front shoe and the two sets of rear shoes needs to be adjusted so that while each brake drum is not binding and is free to turn it is only just free to turn. When the braking system is otherwise in perfect order, it is excessive brake shoe to drum clearance that causes excessive brake pedal travel on Minis. Expect to have to adjust the shoes on drum brake Minis quite frequently and, if the car's brakes are really used hard, expect to have to replace the brake shoes annually.

What is often not realised is that brake shoes (especially new ones) frequently 'settle' after a few miles/kilometres and that one or two further clicks of adjustment might well be possible, giving a 'hard' pedal well within the first 1in/25mm of pedal travel from rest. With the standard componentry it doesn't get any better than this. It takes a little bit of time to set up the Mini drum brake system but attention to detail will pay dividends.

It really is a good idea to check the adjustment of the brake shoes every three months on a brake drum-equipped Mini. It does not take too much shoe wear for the pedal travel to start increasing before the brakes start to work. Setting each brake drum so that the drum can rotate freely (just) is the optimum. The rear brakes have 90 degree turn setting, which allows the brake shoes to be adjusted to within one click of either allowing free rotation of the wheel, or the wheel binding. The front brakes have adjusters which allow the shoes to be brought very close to the drums.

Another factor which affects brake performance is brake dust. As the shoes wear, dust collects in the drum and around the back plate. The amount of dust floating around inside the brake drum can become quite considerable and be the cause of the most dreadful grinding noise when the brakes are applied. The solution is quite simple: remove the brake drums and thoroughly clean the drums and back plates, around the wheel cylinders and brake linings. A 1in/25mm paint brush is often the best thing to use to sweep off the brake dust. The lining faces might well need to be lightly sanded to remove the build up of dust compacted on them. Clear brake dust annually. Softer standard type replacement brake shoe linings are more prone to creating the brake dust

problem than harder competition linings.

DRUM BRAKE SYSTEM MODIFICATIONS
Finned aluminium drums

For weekend club racing, or when a serious improvement in braking is required while retaining drum brakes, the following mods work well. Harder than standard brake shoes (Ferodo EG 95, or similar) front and rear and 'MiniFin' brake drums fitted to the front brakes. What the excellent MiniFins (or similar products) do is to get rid of the heat generated by braking as quickly as possible. Not only is aluminium much better at dissipating heat than cast iron, but these MiniFin brake drums have a large number of fins to increase the overall surface area exposed to air and therefore get rid of the generated heat three or four times as quickly as the standard cast iron drums can. Having two MiniFin brake drums on the front of any drum braked Mini is a good idea.

When heat is continually applied to cast iron drums by the friction of hard braking they heat up and expand. The shoes then have to move out further to remain in firm contact and, eventually, they run out of travel and the brakes fade. It can even get to the point where the driver can feel the brakes 'going' as - no matter how hard the pedal is pushed - the car will not slow and the brake linings will likely start to deteriorate by this stage (burning smell). The same brake system fitted with MiniFin-type brake drums will eventually fail, but takes some provocation, especially if cooling ducts are fitted to funnel cool air from the front of the car and duct it to the outer finned surface of each front brake drum. It does take a fair bit of work to duct air correctly to the front brake drums, but it can be done and is

well worth the effort.

Rear brakes can be left as per standard in most instances as most of the braking on Minis is done by the front brakes (about 75-80 per cent). MiniFin-type brake drums are also available for the rear brakes if required.

Rear brakes

The rear brakes on some Minis have a tendency to lock up under hard braking or during an emergency stop. This will have the effect of either causing the car to 'slew' to one side, quite violently in some instances, with the car needing steering correction, or go straight ahead with one or both rear wheels locked up. Either way, the situation is dangerous.

This problem is usually caused by the rear brake bias valve being faulty. On older cars, the piston inside the unit ends up jammed and unable to move to shut off the oil supply to the rear brake cylinders at the predetermined line pressure. Full line pressure goes then to the rear brakes and they lock instantly. The early bias valves are non-serviceable, and a complete new replacement unit will have to be fitted.

The circuitry of the early type of brake bias valve (fitted onto the rear sub-frame) works on the principle that the circuit is open when the system is static (the brake pedal is not being touched) and when it just comes under line pressure. The circuit then remains open until a predetermined amount of line pressure is reached, at which point the mechanism inside the valve shuts off. This means that the line pressure that has been generated by the driver pushing down the brake pedal and operating the rear brakes, is 'trapped' in the system past the valve (and remains constant until the brake pedal is released). That line pressure is maintained, even though the line pressure in the rest of the braking system (that is, going to the front brakes and the brake line that goes to the primary side of the rear bias valve) could double.

When the braking system comes under pressure, a piston inside the bias valve starts to move (a distance commensurate with the amount of line pressure being generated). When the piston reaches the limit of its travel, the hydraulic oil under pressure is shut off, and cannot pass into the rear brake lines. The factor which controls the rate of piston movement and the valve shut off point is the spring, located behind the piston, which resists the line pressure acting on the top of the piston. The lighter the spring, the quicker the valve will shut off, and, conversely, the stronger the spring, the more line pressure will be required to shut the valve off.

If the braking system is in perfect working order and the rear brakes still lock up, the spring tension is too high and needs to be reduced. If the rear wheels can't be locked up, the rear brake bias valve could be working perfectly but have insufficient spring tension. The only way of knowing whether it's correct or not, is to increase the spring pressure until the brakes lock up. At that point you know for sure that there is too much line pressure getting through to the rear brakes. Spring substitution is an obvious method for adjusting the original equipment brake bias valve (check with a vehicle testing station, or the DVLA in the UK, that spring substitution is legal). An aftermarket adjustable rear brake bias valve is really the answer and they are not overly expensive.

Adjustable rear brake bias valves

work on exactly the same principle, but with the spring pressure altered via its fitted height (using a multi-position lever or an infinite adjusting screw).

Because of the large number of different sized wheels and tyres fitted to Minis, the standard rear brake bias valve may no longer be calibrated exactly to suit your particular Mini. If you have very wide tyres on your car, for example, the rear will very likely have too much braking on it. An adjustable brake bias valve will cure this problem. Check the legality (from the point of view of your insurance) of fitting a non-standard, adjustable valve.

Another problem that can occur here is that the rear trailing arms becomes seized (fixed in position) due to years of not being greased at the correct intervals. This usually happens on one side of the rear of the car. What happens is that, the instant the brakes are applied, the front of the car pitches forward slightly, as normal, but only one trailing arm drops down at the rear of the car. The wheel of the seized trailing arm lifts accordingly, and has reduced wheel weight on it, while the wheel on the other side maintains, by comparison, an amount of wheel weight. The wheel of the seized trailing arm locks/skids due to the effectively reduced and unequal weight acting on the wheels, and the car will 'slew' wildly. Keep the trailing arms well greased, and check them every six months to see that they are free to move up and down as they should.

Disc brakes

Optimising the drum brake braking system as has been described goes a long way to improving a Mini's braking performance to a level acceptable to

most people who increase their Mini's performance as described in this book. However, realistically, only disc brakes and a well adjusted braking system in first class condition will provide the best braking performance.

It was not until 1984 that volume production Minis came with decent brakes (8.4in diameter disc brakes fitted as standard). This change coincided with the fitting of 12in wheels which were required for caliper clearance. The brakes were then essentially excellent, and especially so for a standard road car.

The change from a 10in wheel and tyre to a 12in wheel and tyre resulted in an approximate 1in increase in tyre diameter (from 18.5in to 19.5in approximately). This had minimal impact on road speed, but it did make a difference. A Mini which had a 3.4 to 1 final drive ratio, for example, would do approximately 80mph at 5000rpm on 10in wheels. After a change to 12in wheels, however, that same car would do approximately 84.3mph, which is an increase in the miles per hour per 1000rpm of the engine from 16.0 to 16.85. A Mini which had a 3.105 to 1 final drive ratio, for example, would do approximately 88.7mph at 5000rpm on 10in wheels. After a change to 12in wheels, that same car would do approximately 93.7mph, an increase in miles per hour per 1000rpm of the engine from 17.73 to 18.7. It's a good way of increasing the miles per hour per 1000rpm of engine speed.

Avoid fitting wheels with large amounts of offset, though, as they cause poor handling characteristics (it becomes difficult to steer the car, and difficult to control it over bumps) even if they make the car look better.

Postscript

One day, a tatty but low mileage 1983 Mini City came into the workshop, and it was decided to modify the engine using some of the old parts we had lying around. The engine was in a very good mechanical condition, and the miles, at about 35,000, were genuine. The car went just as you'd expect a 998cc car to go with a 2.9 to 1 final drive.

The cylinder head was removed, revealing no bore wear of any description, and a very clean '295' casting cylinder head, which had been planed by 0.080in/2.0mm, was fitted (with a new cylinder head gasket, of course). This cylinder head had been fitted with stronger valve springs than standard by a previous owner. The camshaft was replaced with a BP 300/2 Piper one which, although not new one, was in good condition. The only reason this camshaft was used was because it was there at the time. A new single row timing chain was also fitted.

The distributor was replaced with one of my modified Ducellier ones. This had 10 degrees of mechanical advance, and springs which allowed full advance to be achieved at about 2800-3000rpm. The distributor was timed for 35 degrees of total advance, which meant that the engine had 15 degrees of static advance. The vacuum advance had been removed.

A reasonably new complete RC 40 single box exhaust system was fitted, as was a 40mm sidedraught Weber carburettor, with one of those 'goose neck' inlet manifolds. I checked the Weber, but it was pretty much left as found. That's as far as the engine alterations went, with the next step being to tune the carburettor. The engine went well from the start, but it was improved over the course of the day.

We couldn't really have done much less to improve the engine, but the results were quite astounding. In fact, I can't think of another time

when such a small-engined car has surprised me by its performance. The transformation was quite startling, and the car was really quite brilliant to drive, not very different to the 1275cc cars we'd had over the years which had a lot on money spent on them. The drum brakes were quite hopeless, of course, and the car was quite dangerous really, but we were all very careful when driving it.

I don't know what the top speed was, but, after we'd put a rev counter in the car, we discovered a natural tendency to change gear at about 7000-7500rpm (when the power surge slowed). The car did about 10-15 miles to the gallon, and was really quite unsuitable for everyday driving.

The 998cc engine became my favourite Mini engine from that day on. I can't remember what happened to that car now, but whenever I think of a Mini I liked, that one, and one 1275cc car, out of about 25 that I dealt with over a five year period, always come to mind. The orange painted 1275 with the downdraught IDA Weber received similar treatment to the 998, and was the best of the lot. The body on this car was also in a poor condition.

We were, of course, confined to straight line work because, without a central oil pickup pipe, no cornering of any consequence is possible. To fit this is a major job, of course, but it's not impossible to ruin the main and big end bearings of a Mini on a reasonably large roundabout, or so I'm told!

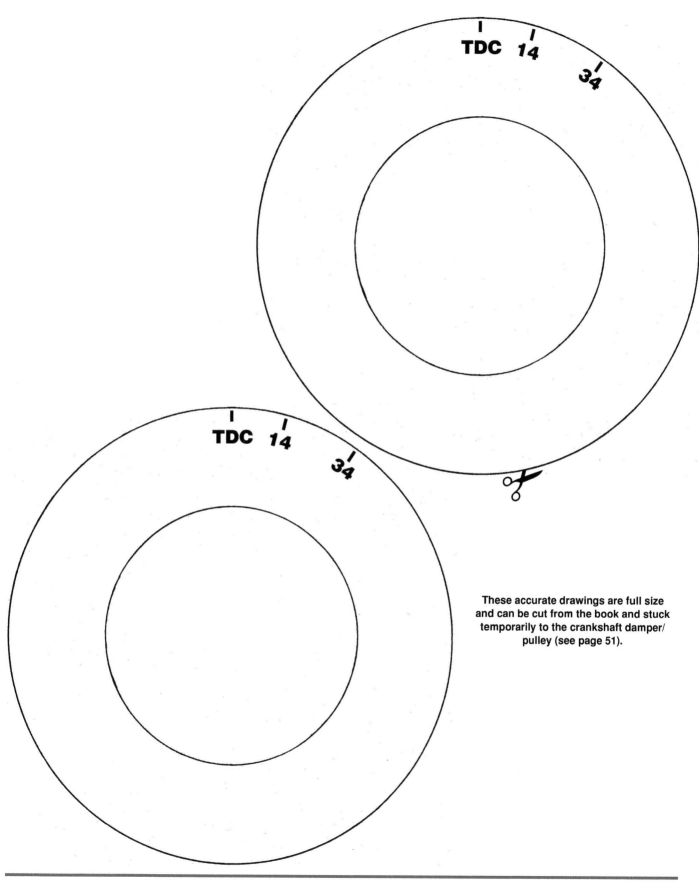

These accurate drawings are full size and can be cut from the book and stuck temporarily to the crankshaft damper/pulley (see page 51).

Expert practical advice from an experienced race engine builder on how to build an ignition system that delivers maximum power reliably. A lot is talked about ignition systems, and there is a bewildering choice of expensive aftermarket parts, which all claim to deliver more power. Des Hammill cuts through the myth and hyperbole, and tells readers what really works, so that they can build an excellent system without wasting money on parts and systems that simply don't deliver. Ignition timing and advance curves for modified engines is another minefield for the inexperienced, but Des uses his expert knowledge to tell readers how to optimise the ignition timing of any high-performance engine.The book applies to all four-stroke gasoline/petrol engines with distributor-type ignition systems, including those using electronic ignition modules: it does not cover engines controlled by ECUs (electronic control units).

ISBN: 978-1-84584-186-7
Paperback • 25x20.7cm • 80 pages
• 98 colour and b&w pictures

All you could want to know about the most famous and popular high performance sidedraught carbs. Covers strip and rebuild, tuning, choke sizes and much more.

ISBN: 978-1-903706-75-6
Paperback • 25x20.7cm • 128 pages
• 181 colour and b&w pictures

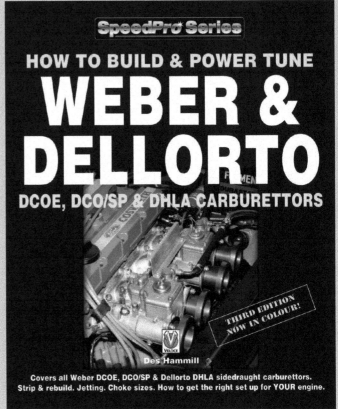

For more information and price details, visit our website at
www.veloce.co.uk
• email: **info@veloce.co.uk**
• Tel: **+44(0)1305 260068**

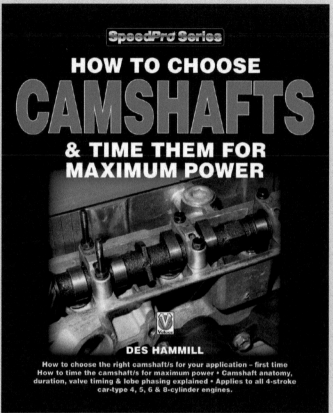

How to choose the right camshaft or camshafts for your individual application. Takes the mystery out of camshaft timing and tells you how to obtain optimum timing for maximum power. Applies to all four-stroke car-type engines.

**ISBN: 978-1-903706-59-6
Paperback • 25x20.7cm • 64 pages
• 95 colour and b&w pictures**

The complete practical guide to successfully modifying classic/retro 2-valve cylinder heads for maximum power, economy and reliability. Applies to almost every car/motorcycle (not 2-stroke) and to all road and track applications.

**ISBN: 978-1-903706-76-3
Paperback • 25x20.7cm • 112 pages
• 150+ b&w pictures**

Index